*M*ARRIAGES

of

*L*AWRENCE *C*OUNTY,

*T*ENNESSEE

1818-1854

Compiled by
EDYTHE RUCKER WHITLEY

Baltimore
GENEALOGICAL PUBLISHING CO., INC.
1982

Introduction

AWRENCE COUNTY was erected in 1817 from parts of Hickman and Maury counties and named in honor of James Lawrence, Captain of the *Chesapeake*, who was famous for his cry "Don't give up the ship!"

About 1815 a grain mill, a distillery, and a Primitive Baptist Church were established near Henryville on the Big Buffalo River. From this time the population increased rapidly, and within a few years Lawrence County was fairly thriving. Prominent among the early settlers were the Parkes, Stribling, Sykes, Simms, and Bentley families. David Crockett arrived in the county soon after its settlement and lived there for several years. He was a member of the County Court and of the building committee that erected the first courthouse. The early records of Lawrence County, notably the marriage records, date from this period.

The marriage bonds and licenses abstracted in the first section of this book were not originally recorded in a register. In recent years they were recorded in a marriage record book and are now on file in the county clerk's office in Lawrenceburg. The later records, those in Section 2, are on file in the same office.

The first section of this work, covering the years 1818 to 1838, contains records of both bonds and licenses. The reader is reminded that a bond alone is not proof of marriage, only that marriage was intended. In Section 2, which covers the years 1838 to 1854, the first date given in each entry is the date the bond or license was issued. The date following (in parentheses) is the date the marriage was performed. If a second date is not given, then the single date provided refers merely to the date of issue of the bond or license.

Edythe Rucker Whitley
Nashville, Tennessee

LAWRENCE COUNTY, TENNESSEE

Marriages, 1818-1854

Section 1: Bonds and Licenses, 1818-1838

Adams, James & Candis Clifton, Jul. 10, 1830 (Bond).
Bennett Wallace, BM.
Adams, James & Candis Clifton, Jul. 10, 1830 (Lic.).
Jul. 21, 1830.
Adams, William C. & Eliza S. Irby, Apr. 1, 1830 (Bond).
William McKnight, Jr., BM.
Alderson, William B. & Anny Edwards, Apr. 19, 1819
(Bond). Henry Sharp, BM.
Alderson, William B. & Anny Sharp, Apr. 19, 1819 (Lic.).
Apr. 19, 1819.
Alexander, Harvey A. & Mahaley Alford, Dec. 29, 1829
(Lic.). Dec. 29, 1829.
Alford, Isaac W. & Mary P. Edmiston, Jul. 26, 1831
(Bond). Franklin Buchanan, BM.
Allison, Samuel & Mary Comer, Jan. 23, 1830 (Lic.).
Jan. 26, 1830.
Allsup, Anderson & Ealinor Springer, Oct. 1821 (Bond).
Elijah Springer, BM.
Alvis, Ashley & Esther Elizabeth Edmiston, Nov. 15, 1833
(Bond). Lemuel B. Denton, BM.
Alvis, Woodford & Luvina Sullivan, Feb. 17, 1827 (Lic.).
Feb. 18, 1827.
Anderson, Aaron & Clary Canon, May 8, 1820 (Bond).
William Swain, BM.
Anderson, John & Peggy Cook, Apr. 9, 1828 (Bond).
William Marcum, BM.
Anthony, John Lewallen & Mary Voss, Mar. 7, 1836 (Bond).
A. M. Perkins, BM.
Anthony, John Allen & Mary Voss, Mar. 7, 1836 (Lic.).
Mar. 7, 1836.
Anthony, John M. & Christiana Boshiers, Oct. 30, 1834
(Bond). John Burris, BM.
Anthony, John M. & Christiana Boshiers, Oct. 30, 1834
(Lic.). Oct. 30, 1834.
Appleton, Rial J. & Elizabeth Snodgrass, Sep. 20, 1835
(Bond). Hiram F. Appleton, BM.

1

Archer, Berry & Marcum Pearce, Nov. 24, 1825 (Bond).
Merrill Archer, BM.
Archer, Daniel & Polly Bird, Jan. 30, 1827 (Bond).
W. W. Matthews, BM.
Archer, Daniel & Jane Cannon, Aug. 24, 1829 (Bond).
Aaron Saunders, BM.
Archer, George & Elizabeth Isaacs, Apr. 30, 1829 (Lic.
returned "Unexecuted").
Archer, George & Elizabeth Miller, Jun. 12, 1829 (Lic.).
Archer, Thomas & Pernia Lyons, Apr. 19, 1832 (Bond).
William Byrd, BM.
Archer, Thomas & Pernia Lyons, Apr. 19, 1832 (Lic.).
Apr. 19, 1832.
Arnold, Edward & Elizabeth Nickson, Aug. 29, 1836 (Bond).
Robert Lince, BM.
Arnold, Edward & Elizabeth Nickson, Aug. 29, 1836 (Lic.).
Aug. 31, 1836.
Arnold, George H. & Elizabeth E. Stewart, Apr. 23, 1834
(Lic.).
Arp, Luke & Elizabeth Gray, Apr. 1818 (Bond). Ebenezer
Thompson, BM.
Arp, Luke & Elizabeth Gray, Apr. 12, 1818 (Lic.).
Ashmore, John C. & Polly Rea, Mar. 13, 1824 (Bond).
Daniel Buie, BM.
Ashmore, John C. & Polly Rea, Mar. 13, 1824 (Lic.).
Mar. 13, 1824.
Ashmore, John C. & Letty Ray, Mar. 26, 1827 (Bond).
John S. Hillhouse, BM.
Askew, James & Nancy Null, Jul. 4, 1821 (Bond). William
Green, BM.
Atkins, Lewis L. & Elizabeth Day, Dec. 21, 1826 (Lic.).
Dec. 21, 1826.
Atwell, William & Lurany Manuel, Aug. 14, 1837 (Bond).
John G. Durbin, BM.
Atwell, William & Lurany Manuel, Aug. 14, 1837 (Lic.).
Aug. 14, 1837.

Bailey, George & Elizabeth Rackley, Mar. 10, 1838 (Bond).
James McIntyre, BM.
Bailey, George & Elizabeth Rackley, Mar. 10, 1838 (Lic.).
Mar. 11, 1838.
Bailey, Samuel S. & Aggy Rackley, Mar. 21, 1829 (Bond).
J. H. Bailey, BM.
Bailey, Samuel S. & Aggy Rackley, Mar. 21, 1829 (Lic.).
Mar. 22, 1829.
Baitman, Esau & Betsey James, Sep. 26, 1833 (Bond).
Cossen C. Anderson, BM.
Baker, James L. & Martha A. Wasson, Feb. 19, 1835 (Bond).
Thomas McRory, BM.
Baker, James L. & Martha A. Wasson, Feb. 19, 1835 (Lic.).
Feb. 18, 1835.
Baker, Larkin & Spicy Hill, Nov. 6, 1821 (Bond).
Anonymous Irvine, BM.

Ball, Johnathan & Sally Pickard, Jun. 4, 1823 (Lic.).
    Jun. 5, 1823.
Barefoot, Dillen & Nancy Choat, Apr. 3, 1818 (Lic.).
    Apr. 3, 1818.
Barnett, Charles & Sarah Welch, Jan. 14, 1836 (Bond).
    James M. Bumpass, BM.
Barnett, Charles & Sarah Welch, Jan. 14, 1836 (Lic.).
    Jan. 17, 1836.
Barr, Nathan & Martha Cottrell, Oct. 12, 1831 (Bond).
    Ephraim Barnett, BM.
Bassham, Drury & Rebecca Brashears, Aug. 5, 1831 (Bond).
    Alexander Brashears, BM.
Bassham, Drury & Rebecca Brashears, Aug. 5, 1831 (Lic.).
    Jul. 17, 1831.
Bassham, Johnston & Sady Poteet, Sep. 3, 1833 (Bond).
    Levi R. Poteet, BM.
Bassham, Richard & Moarning Moody (Reed), Jun. 14, 1821
    (Lic.). June 14, 1821.
Beck, Micajah & Elizabeth Green, Dec. 30, 1837 (Bond).
    Moses Tomblin, BM.
Belew, Ramsey & Rebecca Johnston, Dec. 27, 1823 (Bond).
    Mises Micke, BM.
Belew, Ramsey & Rebecca Johnston, Dec. 27, 1823 (Lic.).
    Dec. 28, 1823.
Bell, John & Eliza J. Duncan, Jun. 30, 1838 (Bond).
    A.W, Hagan, BM.
Bell, John & Eliza J. Duncan, Jun. 30, 1838 (Lic.).
    Jul. 1, 1838.
Bell, Leander & Elizabeth Humphries, Aug. 4, 1830 (Bond).
    Joshua Barber, BM.
Bentley, Daniel & Matilda Lindsey, May 15, 1822 (Bond).
    James Forgey, BM.
Bird, Thomas T. & Sady Down, Apr. 15, 1818 (Bond).
    Samuel Poteet, BM.
Bird, William & Rebecca Archer, May 6, 1829 (Bond).
    Adam Brazier, BM.
Bird, William & Rebecca Archer, May 6, 1829 (Lic.).
    May 10, 1829.
Bishop, Alfred & Milley Day, Oct. 15, 1835 (Bond).
    William Counts, BM.
Bishop, James R. & Elizabeth Price, Mar. 11, 1834 (Lic.).
    Mar. 11, 1834.
Bishop, Joseph & Nancy Brashears, Jun. 18, 1837 (Bond).
    Peter Brashears, BM.
Blackburn, Benjamin & Mary Eddins, Oct. 7, 1835 (Lic.).
    Oct. 7, 1835.
Blair, Thomas & Sara Cunningham, Oct. 30, 1823 (Bond).
Blair, Thomas & Sara Cunningham, Oct. 30, 1823 (Lic.).
    Oct. 30, 1823.
Blair, Thomas & Elizabeth McLaren, Jun. 2, 1834 (Lic.).
    Oct. 9, 1834.
Blythe, Lemuel & Nelly Spencer, Aug. 5, 1819 (Bond).
    Ambrose Spencer, BM.
Blythe, Lemuel & Nelly Spencer, Aug. 5, 1819 (Lic.).
    Aug. 5, 1819.

Boren, Absolem & Harriet Pearce, Aug. 27, 1833 (Bond).
Alford Bird, BM.
Boren, George W. & Rachel Davis, Aug. 30, 1837 (Bond).
James W. Davis.
Bowden, Charles W. & Elvira Lysle, Sep. 20, 1838 (Bond).
George W. Franks, BM.
Bowden, Charles W. & Elvira Lysle, Sep. 20, 1838 (Lic.).
Sep. 20, 1838.
Bowden, James & Elizabeth McAnally, Mar. 12, 1838 (Bond).
William Bowden, BM.
Bowdry, Joshua & Jane Simonton, Jul. 23, 1829 (Bond).
F. Buchanan, BM.
Bowdry, Joshua & Jane Simonton, Jul. 23, 1829 (Lic.).
Jul. 23, 1829.
Brashears, Berry & Frances Pryor, Aug. 13, 1836 (Lic.).
Aug. 13, 1836.
Brashears, Isaac & Mary Bassham, Dec. 4, 1833 (Bond).
Walter Brashears, BM.
Brashears, Jesse & Elizabeth Bell, Mar. 2, 1818 (Bond).
Nathan Brashears, BM.
Brashears, John & Oma Hogg, Mar. 2, 1831 (Bond). William
Hughs, BM.
Brashears, Pete & Bicy Brazhears, Feb. 9, 1835 (Bond).
Basil Brashears, BM.
Brashears, Thomas & Polly Sullivant, Jan. 12, 1836 (Bond).
Basil Brashears, BM.
Brazil, Reubin & Catharine McDougal, Oct. 13, 1836 (Bond).
Hugh C. McIntyre, BM.
Brewer, Elias & Leticia Wallace, May 18, 1836 (Bond).
Timothy Wallace, BM.
Brewer, Elias & Leticia Wallace, May 18, 1836 (Lic.).
May 18, 1836.
Brewer, George & Catharine Linam, Sep. 18, 1823 (Bond).
Thomas Spencer, BM.
Brewer, George & Martha Sessums, Mar. 28, 1838 (Lic.).
Apr. 1, 1838.
Brewer, Jackson & Julian Markham, Feb. 14, 1835 (Lic.).
Feb. 19, 1835.
Brewer, Joseph & Elizabeth E. Roberson, Jan. 5, 1837
(Lic.). Jan. 19, 1837.
Brewer, John H. & Sarah Holloway, Feb. 27, 1838 (Bond).
Jackson K. Bowden, BM.
Brewer, John H. & Sarah Holloway, Feb. 27, 1838 (Lic.).
Feb. 27, 1838.
Brewer, Julius & Margaret Gist, Oct. 3, 1820 (Lic.).
Oct. 5, 1820.
Brown, John F. & Anna Wyrick, May 24, 1838 (Bond).
Samuel L. Duffield, BM.
Brown, John F. & Anna Wyrick, May 24, 1838 (Lic.).
May 26, 1838.
Brown, Samuel & Zilphy McCareby, Jan. 9, 1824 (Bond).
Lucas Walker, BM.
Brumley, Isaac & Polly Archer, Mar. 2, 1836 (Lic.).
Mar. 2, 1836.

Brumley, James & Patsey Barnett, Oct. 1, 1823 (Bond).
Larkin Brumley, BM.
Brumley, Jesse & Sarah Hutcheson, Mar. 12, 1838 (Lic.).
Mar. 12, 1838.
Brumley, William & Mary Hutcheson, Feb. 16, 1826 (Bond).
Jesse Sims, BM.
Brumley, William & Mary Hutcheson, Feb. 16, 1826 (Lic.).
Feb. 16, 1826.
Bryan, John & Milley Pullin, Sep. 21, 1831 (Bond).
Jacob Bryan, BM.
Bryant, Elihu & Sophia Williamson, Nov. 25, 1836 (Bond).
Coonrod Hartwick, BM.
Bryant, Needham & Jane Null, Mar. 7, 1821 (Lic.).
Mar. 7, 1821.
Buchanan, Franklin & Adelaide Simonton, Feb. 10, 1831
(Lic.). Feb. 10, 1831.
Bunpass, A.W. & Eleanor Buchanan, Dec. 2, 1822 (Lic.).
Dec. 3, 1822.
Bunpass, E.L. & Elizabeth Henry, Aug. 5, 1829 (Bond).
John B. Morrow, BM.
Bumpass, J.B. & Frances D. Linam, Jul. 5, 1828 (Bond).
Douglas H. Stockton, BM.
Bumpass, J.B. & Frances D. Linam, Jul. 5, 1828 (Lic.).
Jul. 9, 1828.
Burks, Claiborne & Letitha Singleton, Jun. 1, 1838 (Lic.).
Jun. 1, 1838.
Burlison, Hilkien & Celia Burlison, Sep. 15, 1834 (Bond).
B. Halford, BM.
Burlison, Hilray & Scily Odom, Feb. 4, 1833 (Lic.).
Feb. 4, 1833.
Burlison, James & Polly Holland, Feb. 1, 1832 (Lic.).
Feb. 1, 1832.
Burlison, John & Milley Grenaway, May 26, 1834 (Lic.).
May 26, 1834.
Burns, Aquilla & Elizabeth Griffin, Oct. 1, 1818 (Bond).
William Welch, BM.
Burns, Berryman & E. Heralston, Nov. 3, 1823 (Bond).
Jacob Matthews, BM.
Burns, Berryman & Cyrena Pennington, Mar. 1, 1826 (Bond).
Jacob Matthews, BM.
Burns, Laird & Waldrop Lurnany, Dec. 3, 1818 (Bond).
James Burns, BM.
Burns, William & Amy Wallis, Apr. 21, 1821 (Lic.).
Jul. 3, 1821.
Burris, Richard & Elvire Brownlow, Jun. 1, 1832.
Burris, Richard & Sally Rodgers, Jul. 27, 1832 (Bond).
Elijah Melton, BM.
Burris, Richard & Sally Rodgers, Jul. 27, 1832 (Lic.).
Jul. 29, 1832.
Burris, William & Catharine Davis, Nov. 15, 1835 (Lic.).
Nov. 15, 1835.
Burris, William C. & Deely H. Wiggs, Oct. 26, 1836 (Bond).
Rial J. Roberts, BM.

LAWRENCE COUNTY MARRIAGES

Butler, Anderson & Patsey Smith, Feb. 27, 1826 (Lic.).
  Mar. 2, 1826.
Butler, Asa & Milly L. Layton, Sep. 22, 1835 (Bond).
  Robert Dial, BM.
Byrd, Holdman & Caroline M. Willis, Jun. 12, 1829 (Bond).
  Jacob Bird, BM.
Byrd, Jacob & Mary Standridge, Dec. 5, 1834 (Lic.).
  Dec. 11, 1834.
Cabe, William & Nancy Stags, Dec. 2, 1818 (Bond).
  David Crockett, BM.
Callahan, John J. & Sarah Ann Ezell, Nov. 19, 1835 (Bond).
  Edmund D. Ezell, BM.
Callahan, John J. & Sarah Ann Ezell, Nov. 19, 1835 (Lic.).
  Nov. 27, 1835.
Campbell, Alexander & Alsey Bumpass, Jul. 1, 1824 (Bond).
  Allen Campbell, BM.
Campbell, Allen E. & Flora Patterson, Aug. 30, 1827 (Bond).
  Archibald W. Blue, BM.
Campbell, Daniel & Amy McIntyre, Aug. 22, 1825 (Lic.).
  Aug. 22, 1825.
Campbell, Hugh & Nancy McDonald, Apr. 7, 1818 (Bond).
  Edmund Bailey, BM.
Canon, James & Temperance Thomas, Dec. 19, 1838 (Lic.).
  Dec. 22, 1836.
Carswell, George & Arilla McCafferty, Oct. 7, 1829 (Bond).
  D.H. Stockton, BM.
Carter, Andrew & Margaret Haggins, Feb. 12, 1830 (Bond).
  John G. McDonald, BM.
Carter, James & Sary Perremore, Feb. 10, 1830 (Bond).
  Vincant Carter, BM.
Carter, James H. & Elizabeth J. Richardson, Dec. 6, 1838
  (Bond). Dec. 6, 1838.
Casey, John & Elizabeth Hartwick, Oct. 23, 1834 (Lic.).
  Oct. 26, 1834.
Casey, Samuel H. & Lycretia B. Cayce, Aug. 15, 1833 (Bond).
  Levi McDonald, BM.
Cayce, D. (?) N. & Matildy Gaither, Jan. 12, 1837 (Bond).
  E.N. Lindsey, BM.
Cayce, D.N. & Matildy Gaither, Jan. 12, 1837 (Lic.).
  Jan. 12, 1837.
Cerat, George & Lucinda Brashears, Feb. 9, 1828 (Bond).
  Berry Brashears, BM.
Chaffin, David & Jane Deason, May 26, 1839 (Bond).
  James McMillin, BM.
Chaffin, David & Jane Deason, May 26, 1832 (Lic.).
  May 29, 1832.
Chaffin, James & Anne M. Turner, Feb. 19, 1829 (Bond).
  James May, BM.
Chaffin, John & (Name not shown), Mar. 22, 1820 (Bond).
  Nathaniel Mason, BM.
Chaffin, John & Elizabeth Williams, Mar. 18, 1830 (Lic.).
  Mar. 18, 1830.
Chaffin, William & Mahala Johns, Oct. 18, 1823 (Bond).
  Joseph P. Crosthwaite, BM.

LAWRENCE COUNTY MARRIAGES

Chambers, Berry & Jane Buford, Jan. 9, 1830 (Bond).
John Voss, BM.
Chambers, James & Caroline Linum, Aug. 7, 1837 (Lic.).
Aug. 7, 1837.
Chambers, John & Anna Bowden, Nov. 27, 1828 (Bond).
Stephen Matthews, BM.
Chapman, James C. & Martha Petty, Jun. 7, 1838 (Lic.).
Jun. 7, 1838.
Chapman, Steadman A. & Sarah McQuigg, Sep. 27, 1834
(Bond). A.T. McQuigg, BM.
Charry, Willis W. & Frances E. Weir, Jul. 31, 1828 (Bond).
William Henry, BM.
Cherry, Willis W. & Francis E. Weir, Jul. 31, 1828 (Lic.).
Jul. 31, 1828.
Choldress, Joseph & Susannah York, Dec. 24, 1825 (Lic.).
Feb. 5, 1826.
Choat, Stockly & Prudy Choat, Dec. 30, 1823 (Bond).
James Choat, BM.
Choat, James & Elizabeth Heralson, Sep. 14, 1824 (Bond).
Robert Heralson, BM.
Choat, Thomas & Susannah Dalton, Dec. 15, 1832 (Lic.).
Dec. 15, 1832.
Chronister, John & Mary Birum, Sep. 10, 1828 (Bond).
William Davis, BM.
Chronister, Phillip & Diannah Heralson, Sep. 3, 1818
(Lic.). Sep. 8, 1818.
Clayton, John & Seneth Wallis, Aug. 28, 1837 (Lic.).
Aug. 31, 1837.
Clayton, William & Charrity Gower, Aug. 15, 1828 (Lic.).
Aug. 16, 1828.
Clemmons, Henry & Rebecca Curtis, Apr. 18, 1832 (Bond).
Thomas Clemmons, BM.
Clemmons, Henry & Rebecca Curtis, Apr. 18, 1832 (Lic.).
Apr. 20, 1832.
Clifton, James & Cynthian Garner, Nov. 2, 1826 (Lic.).
Nov. 2, 1826.
Clifton, James & Cynthian Garner, Nov. 2, 1826 (Bond).
John Crofford, BM.
Clifton, John & Aseneth Welch, Aug. 19, 1824 (Bond).
Alsey Alford, BM.
Clifton, M.D. & Sarah Wisdom, Jan. 5, 1830 (Bond).
I.W. Alford, BM.
Coble, William & Susa Richie, Oct. 2, 1830 (Bond).
Period Wright, BM.
Cole, Samuel & Nancy Cottrell, Jan. 2, 1824 (Bond).
Samuel Brown, BM.
Cole, Samuel & Nancy Cottrell, Jan. 2, 1824 (Lic.).
Jan. 4, 1824.
Collins, William & Ollivia McFalls, Dec. 31, 1829 (Bond).
Cyrus Bell, BM.
Combs, John S. & Elizabeth Archer, Mar. 30, 1829 (Bond).
A.B. Bailey, BM.
Cook, Hiram & Roseana Anderson, Jul. 9, 1821 (Bond).
Zachus Inman, BM.

7

Cook, Newton & Perny Woods, Sep. 27, 1834 (Bond).
James Cook, BM.
Cook, Newton & Perny Woods, Sep. 27, 1834 (Lic.).
Sep. 30, 1834.
Cooper, Marcum & Sally Hall, Feb. 23, 1825 (Bond).
Basil Sharp, BM.
(?) & Pricilla Pippins, May 12, 1825 (Bond).
Copeland, James C. & Athalinda Ashmore, Nov. 19, 1828
(Bond). George W. Coleburn, BM.
Counce, John & Burthena Bean, May 19, 1819 (Bond).
Moses Spencer, BM.
Counce, John & Burthena Bean, May 17, 1819 (Lic.).
May 18, 1819.
Counce, Wm. C. & Marthy Shackelford, Oct. 13, 1837
Thomas Patterson, BM.
Courtney, Isaac & Lucindy Lane, Jun. 7, 1823 (Lic.).
Jun. 7, 1823.
Cowan, Harvey & Sally Lindsey, Mar. 29, 1824 (Bond).
Jefferson Lindsey, BM.
Cowan, James & Sarah Johnston, Dec. 10, 1838 (Lic.).
Dec. 13, 1838.
Cox, Edmond & Gney Tays, Mar. 26, 1833 (Bond).
Dempsey Odom, BM.
Cox, Edmond & Giney Tays, Mar. 26, 1833 (Lic.).
Apr. 17, 1833.
Craig, David & Catharine Conley, Jan. 5, 1832 (Bond).
Duncan Buie, BM.
Craig, David J. & Mary A. Hunter, Feb. 15, 1831 (Bond).
I.W. Alford, BM.
Craig, James B. & Barbary Vincent, Jun. 1, 1837 (Lic.).
Jun. 1, 1837.
Craig, Johnston & Angeline B. Warren, Dec. 13, 1831
(Lic.). Dec. 15, 1831.
Cranford, John & Martha Linam, Oct. 7, 1823 (Bond).
Jack Clark, BM.
Crews, Thomas & Rosilla W. McMackin, Oct. 2, 1834 (Bond).
Richard Clayton, BM.
Crofford, James P. & Jerry Jane Alvis, Jan. 16, 1822 (Bond).
John A. Hail, BM.
Crofford, James P. & Jerry Jane Alvis, Jan. 16, 1832 (Lic.).
Jan. 16, 1822. (sic)
Crofford, John & Sanny Clifton, Jan. 13, 1826 (Bond).
James Clifton, BM.
Crofford, John & Sanny Clifton, Jan. 13, 1826 (Lic.).
Jan. 14, 1826.
Cromwell, W.F. & Nancy Grimes, Jul. 14, 1825 (Bond).
R.T. Bailey, BM.
Cromwell, W.F. & Nancy Grimes, Jul. 14, 1825 (Lic.).
Jul. 14, 1825.
Cross, Wesley & Anny Green, Dec. 26, 1825 (Bond).
Robt. N. Bell, BM.
Crow, John & Alladelphy Jane (?), Nov. 28, 1828 (Bond).
James Smith, BM.
Culbreth, Daniel & Elizabeth Reed, Nov. 19, 1822 (Lic.).
Jan. 6, 1823.

Cunningham, Eli H. & Sally Ethridge, Jan. 18, 1826 (Bond).
A.W. Bumpass, BM.
Cunningham, Eli H. & Sally Ethridge, Jan. 18, 1826 (Lic.).
Jan. 19, 1826.
Cunningham, James B. & Mary Kilburn, Jan. 26, 1832 (Bond).
Wm. W. Wisdom, BM.
Cunningham, James B. & Mary Kilburn, Jan. 26, 1832 (Lic.).
Jan. 26, 1832.
Curry, James H. & Ealinor Findley, Aug. 13, 1828 (Bond).
Eli McAnally, BM.
Curry, James H. & Ealinor Findley, Aug. 13, 1828 (Lic.).
Aug. 21, 1828.
Dalton, James & Lucy Venable, May 15, 1824 (Bond).
B. Halford, BM.
Dalton, Lewis & Nancy Allen, May 27, 1829 (Lic.).
May 28, 1829.
Dalton, Toliver P. & Eliza P. Cowers, Nov. 19, 1829 (Bond).
Cyrus Bell, BM.
Daniel, Robert C. & Evelina Simpson, Jan. 2, 1838 (Lic.).
Jan. 3, 1838.
Daniel, Theophilus P. & Frances Rochards, Oct. 31, 1833
(Bond). J.C. Carter, BM.
Danley, Andrew & Nancy Burket, Feb. 8, 1825 (Bond).
Wm. Burket, BM.
Davenport, Samuel & Jane Bullidge, Aug. 4, 1818 (Bond).
Lemuel Blythe, BM.
Davidson, George W. & Elizabeth S. Wasson, Oct. 7, 1831
(Lic.). Oct. 7, 1831.
Davis, Benjamin M. & Permelia Lyons, Oct. 31, 1826 (Lic.).
Nov. 2, 1826.
Davis, C.B. & Mary A. Parker, Mar. 30, 1837 (Lic.).
Mar. 30, 1837.
Davis, James & Polly Jeno, Oct. 5, 1831 (Bond).
Moses Winters, BM.
Davis, James & Sally Ward, Aug. 3, 1832 (Bond).
John Davis, BM.
Davis, James & Sally Ward, Apr. 3, 1832 (Lic.).
Apr. 3, 1832.
Davis, James W. & Elizabeth Rosson, Apr. 8, 1837 (Lic.).
Apr. 12, 1837.
Davis, Larkin L. & Rebecca Winters, Aug. 7, 1832 (Lic.).
Aug. 18, 1832.
Davis, Stephen L. & Nancy Brooks, Jan. 5, 1833 (Bond).
Real J. Roberts, BM.
Davis, William & Sarah Simonton, May 26, 1825 (Lic.).
May 26, 1825.
Davis, William & Martha Kilburn, Jan. 21, 1835 (Lic.).
Jan. 22, 1835.
Deavenport, Thomas D. & Mariah Lucus, Jan. 7, 1824 (Bond).
George W. Locke, BM.
Dickson, Thomas C. & Jane White, Jan. 12, 1837 (Bond).
Solomon L. Wood, BM.

LAWRENCE COUNTY MARRIAGES

Dobbins, John E. & Maryan Lewis, Dec. 16, 1832 (Bond).
Robert Hamsley, BM.
Donahoo, Alexander & Charlotte Hinsley, Jul. 8, 1823
(Lic.). Jul. 20, 1823.
Dotson, Ebenezer B. & Angeline Lucus, Nov. 7, 1838
J.B. Kosure, BM.
Douglass, Thomas & Ellen Cooper, Oct. 6, 1831 (Bond).
William Estes, BM.
Duncan, David L. & Elizabeth Sharp, Oct. 5, 1830 (Bond).
A.S. Alexander, BM.
Dunlap, John & Regina DePriest, Mar. 7, 1835 (Lic.).
Mar. 12, 1835.
Durbin, Allen & Amy Fisher, Oct. 22, 1836 (Lic.).
Durbin, John G. & Elizabeth Hartwell, Dec. 15, 1833 (Lic.).
Durbin, Joseph & Nancy Archer, Dec. 11, 1827 (Bond).
Daniel Archer, BM.

Eaton, George & Martha Rackley, Apr. 23, 1829 (Lic.).
Apr. 26, 1829.
Edmiston, Wm. A. & Margaret Dickson, Feb. 1, 1829 (Bond).
A.S. Alexander, BM.
Edwards, Henry C. & Jane A. Day, Nov. 1821 (Lic.).
Nov. 1821.
Edwards, James & Lucinda Aday, Sep. 10, 1834 (Bond).
Stephanis Busby, BM.
Edwards, James & Lucinda Aday, Sep. 10, 1834 (Lic.).
Sep. 10, 1834.
Edwards, William & Telithy Maryman, May 12, 1821 (Bond).
James Maryman, BM.
Edwards, Willie B. & An Jane McDougal, Sep. 7, 1836 (Bond).
David C. Jackson, BM.
Emns, Martin & Anna Brumley, Oct. 9, 1834 (Bond).
R.C. McLaren, BM.
Erwin, Samuel & Sarah Crisp, Mar. 4, 1819 (Bond).
John Crisp, BM.
Erwin, Samuel & Sarah Crisp, Mar. 4, 1819 (Lic.).
Ethridge, William & Lucy Ann T. Flakes, Mar. 4, 1829
(Lic.). Apr. 6, 1829.
Evans, George & Margaret English, Apr. 4, 1824 (Bond).
Am. B. Phillips, BM.
Ezell, Charles G. & Sary Powell, Nov. 19, 1828 (Bond).
M.D. Newton, BM.
Ezell, Danl. & Winney Davis, Aug. 4, 1825 (Lic.).
Aug. 7, 1825.
Ezell, Samuel & Amy Shelton, Oct. 31, 1829 (Bond).
Nathan Barr, BM.

Fanning, Abraham & Nancy Galloway, Jul, 14, 1822 (Bond).
John McClain, Jr., BM.
Fanning, Jacob & Polly Downs, Sep. 24, 1822 (Lic.).
Sep. 24, 1822.
Farmer, Leroy & Nancy Wharton, Nov. 18, 1818 (Bond).
John Smith, BM.

LAWRENCE COUNTY MARRIAGES

Farmer, Leroy & Nancy Wharton, Nov. 18, 1818 (Lic.).
    Nov. 26, 1818.
Finney, John & Sarah Spears, Feb. 19, 1838 (Lic.).
    Feb. 19, 1838.
Fisher, Benjamin & Charity Cooper, Oct. 2, 1829 (Bond).
    William Quillen, BM.
Flake, Chapman & Leedy Futrel, Jul. 1836 (Bond).
    Jacob Brashears, BM.
Floyd, Albert & Mary (Polly) Pollock, Sep. 12, 1829 (Lic.).
    Sep. 15, 1829.
Foldenburg, Leander & Malenda Chapman, Mar. 2, 1837 (Bond).
    Tyree Yates, BM.
Foldenburg, Leander & Malenda Chapman, Mar. 2, 1837 (Lic.).
    Mar. 2, 1837.
Fondren, Henry & Polly Yarbrough, Jan. 7, 1824 (Bond).
    James Parker, BM.
Fondren, John & Nancy McLean, Jun. 26, 1838 (Bond).
    Ezekiel Lindsey, BM.
Fondren, John & Nancy McLean, Jun. 26, 1838 (Lic.).
    Jun. 26, 1838.
Fonville, Jacob R. & Winny Price, Aug. 3, 1833 (Bond).
    Robert Gee, BM.
Forbes, Collin & Elizabeth Sullivant, Sep. 15, 1819 (Lic.).
    Sep. 16, 1819.
Foster, James & Rebecca Rogers, Sep. 28, 1833 (Bond).
    J.H. Blasingam, BM.
Foust, Hyrem & Jane White, Oct. 8, 1833 (Bond).
    Christopher Foust, BM.
Foust, John & Sally Gambrell, May 19, 1829 (Bond).
    Aaron Springer, BM.
Franks, George W. & Anna McAnally, Sep. 25, 1838 (Lic.).
    Sep. 25, 1838.
Franks, Robert & Betsey Harrison, Dec. 19, 1819 (Bond).
    Isaac Courtney, BM.
Fugate, Andrew & Alsey Null, Jul. 28, 1818 (Bond).
    Levi Lewis, BM.

Gaither, Edmond T. & Leticia Beedle, Nov. 15, 1837 (Bond).
    Henry Day, BM.
Gaither, Edmond T. & Leticia Beedle, Nov. 15, 1837 (Lic.).
    Nov. 15, 1837.
Ganbrell, Thomas & Polly (?), Nov. 19, 1820 (Bond).
    John (?), BM.
Garner, Coffee & Mahala White, Mar. 9, 1836 (Bond).
    John Garner, BM.
Garner, Coffee & Mahala White, Mar. 9, 1836 (Lic.).
    Mar. 10, 1836.
Gatewood, William & Angeline Duncan, Aug. 12, 1826 (Bond).
    William Hall, BM.
Gatlin, Edmund & Elizabeth Boswell, Dec. 23, 1830 (Bond).
    John G. McDonald, BM.
Gauge, James & Nancy Webster, Feb. 19, 1820 (Bond).
    James Webster, BM.
Gee, Thomas & Elizabeth Hammons, May 29, 1818 (Bond).
    Henry Hammons, BM.

11

LAWRENCE COUNTY MARRIAGES

George, William & Sally Rowland, Jul. 15, 1818 (Lic.).
Jul. 15, 1818.
Gibson, James J. & Mary J. Lucas, Oct. 11, 1837 (Bond).
Thomas L. Porter, BM.
Gilbert, Davis & Polly Davis, Sep. 15, 1827 (Bond).
Barnabas ("Barney") Gabel, BM.
Gilbert, Davis & Polly Davis, Sep. 15, 1827 (Lic.).
Sep. 16, 1827.
Gilbert, William R. & Louise Foster, Jul. 4, 1836 (Bond).
Robert Flake, BM.
Gilbert, William R. & Louise Foster, Jul. 4, 1836 (Lic.).
Jul. 7, 1836.
Gill, Gardner T. & Elizabeth Flournoy, Sep. 3, 1818
(Bond). Nathaniel Mason, BM.
Gist, Joseph & Sinah Hollis, May 22, 1818 (Bond).
Ezer Evans, BM.
Glover, John & Caroline Lumpkins, Aug. 1, 1832 (Bond).
Levi Boswell, BM.
Glover, John & Caroline Lumpkins, Aug. 1, 1832 (Lic.).
Aug. 2, 1832.
Glover, William & Nancy Fifeny (?), Mar. 8, 1833 (Lic.).
Mar. 8, 1833.
Gordon, Beverley & Nancy Standridge, Sep. 12, 1833 (Bond).
Jeremiah J. Fisher, BM.
Gosnell, Peter & Sally Hoge, Jun. 23, 1827 (Bond).
Benjamin Gosnell, BM.
Gosnell, Peter & Sally Hoge, Jun. 23, 1827 (Lic.).
Jun. 24, 1827.
Gower, Nicholas & Matilda Woodard, Sep. 17, 1829 (Lic.).
Sep. 17, 1829.
Gray, Mark W. & Mar Gwyn, Jun. 6, 1829 (Bond).
James Edmundson, BM.
Green, Allen & Margaret McDougal, Dec. 17, 1838 (Lic.).
Dec. 21, 1838.
Green, Daniel P. & Mailida Montgomery, Sep. 20, 1832
(Lic.). Sep. 21, 1832.
Green, John & Winny Dial, Jan. 16, 1830 (Bond).
William P. Stewart, BM.
Greenhaw, Ephraim B. & Angeline Foster, Sep. 12, 1838
(Lic.). Sep. 12, 1838.
Greenwood, William G. & Catherine Guest, Feb. 15, 1838
(Lic.) Feb. 15, 1838.
Gresham, Andrew & Roena Gibson, Oct. 24, 1835 (Bond).
Thomas N. Thornton, BM.
Gresham, Elijah & Anny Hicks, Aug. 1, 1828 (Lic.).
Aug. 2, 1828.
Gresham, Ephraim & Sarah Choat, Sep. 14, 1831 (Bond).
George Gresham, BM.
Gresham, George & Elizabeth Gordon, Jul. 6, 1835 (Bond).
James P. Hicks, BM.
Gresham, Henry & Inda Johnston, Sep. 23, 1830 (Bond).
G.D. Young, BM.
Gresham, Henry & Eliza Dalton, Oct. 1, 1838 (Bond).
David B. Dalton, BM.

12

LAWRENCE COUNTY MARRIAGES

Gresham, Solomon & Lizza Badchell, Mar. 2, 1820 (Bond).
William F. Cunningham, BM.
Greenhau, William & Susan Jones, Oct. 1, 1838 (Bond).
Edward B. Greenhau, BM.
Grimes, Luke & Polly Null, Nov. 25, 1819 (Lic.).
Nov. 25, 1819.
Grissum, James & Rebecca Phillips, Apr. 7, 1834 (Lic.).
Apr. 7, 1834.
Grissom, James & Elizabeth Blythe, Aug. 15, 1838 (Bond).
George W. Wyrick, BM.
Grissom, James & Elizabeth Blythe, Aug. 15, 1838 (Lic.).
Aug. 15, 1838.

Hagans, John A. & Marian Bumpass, Feb. 19, 1835 (Bond).
Wm. P. Norman, BM.
Hagans, James A. & Marian Bunpass, Feb. 19, 1835 (Lic.).
Feb. 19, 1835.
Hail, Aaron P. & Rutha Lumpkins, May 6, 1837 (Bond).
Robert Kelly, BM.
Hail, Aaron P. & Rutha Lumpkins, May 6, 1837 (Lic.).
May 11, 1837.
Hail, John A. & Martha Sullivant, Mar. 21, 1838 (Lic.).
Mar. 22, 1838.
Hail, Powell E. & Susan Lumpkins, Jan. 8, 1835 (Bond).
Jesse B. Glover, BM.
Hail, Powell E. & Susan Lumpkins, Jan. 8, 1835 (Lic.).
Jan. 8, 1835.
Hamilton, John Hampton & Polly Lucas, Jul. 7, 1819 (Bond).
George Lucus, BM.
Hammonds, Joseph & Susan Hicks, Oct. 25, 1833 (Bond).
John Hicks, BM.
Hammons, Joseph & Susan Hicks, Aug. 25, 1833 (Lic.).
Aug. 25, 1833.
Hammonds, Miles & Nancy Horn, Nov. 7, 1834 (Lic.).
Nov. 9, 1834.
Hammonds, Miles & Eleanor Steen, Mar. 2, 1836 (Lic.).
Mar. 2, 1836.
Harlow, Elza & Martha Pope, May 12, 1834 (Bond).
John B. Day, BM.
Harrelson, Abner & Malinda Geton, Nov. 24, 1830 (Bond).
Phillip Chronister, BM.
Harris, Richard C. & Mary Gyst, May 18, 1831 (Bond).
Lemuel Blythe and Eligah Walker, BM.
Harris, Richard C. & Mary Gyst, May 18, 1831 (Lic.).
May 25, 1831, BM.
Hart, Richard & Mary Dickson, Dec. 24, 1833 (Lic.).
Hartwick, Asa O. & Margaret Stout, Feb. 21, 1838 (Bond).
William Hartwick, BM.
Hartwick, Asa O. & Margaret Stout, Feb. 21, 1838 (Lic.).
Feb. 29, 1838.
Hartwick, Charles & Easter Woods, Aug. 19, 1828 (Lic.).
Oct. 6, 1828.
Hawkins, Wilson & (?) Gray, Jul. 26, 1820 (Bond).
Robert Gray, BM.

Hayes, (?) & Ageline Herrin, Sep. 13, 1833 (Bond).
C.J. Herrin, BM.
Haynes, William & Mary Gideon, Dec. 19, 1837 (Lic.).
Dec. 19, 1837.
Hays, William & Octavia Green, Nov. 17, 1836 (Bond).
Patrick Dial, BM.
Hays, William & Octavia Green, Nov. 17, 1836 (Lic.).
Nov. 17, 1836.
Henderson, Joseph & Betsy Williams, Nov. 24, 1834 (Bond).
James Williams, BM.
Henderson, Joseph & Betsy Williams, Nov. 24, 1834 (Lic.).
Nov. 24, 1834.
Henry, Franklin & Telitha Kanaday, Dec. 9, 1823 (Lic.).
Dec. 9, 1823.
Hensley, John & Sarah Baker, Nov. 24, 1830 (Bond).
Thomas Baker, BM.
Hensley, Russell & Susan Null, Dec. 22, 1826 (Bond).
Alexander Dunahoo, BM.
Hemon (Henson ?), John L. & Jane McKeu, Jul. 7, 1818 (Lic.).
Heraldson, James & Elizabeth Pennington, Sep. 25, 1838
(Bond). William Carrell, BM.
Heraldson, James & Elizabeth Pennington, Sep. 25, 1838
(Lic.). Sep. 25, 1838.
Heralson, Vincent & May Anthony, Apr. 11, 1822 (Lic.).
Hicks, Joseph & Lydia Johns, Dec. 3, 1823 (Bond).
B. Farmer, BM.
Hicks, William C. & Winney Alford, Feb. 14, 1829 (Bond).
James Wasson, BM.
Hicks, William C. & Winney Alford, Feb. 14, 1829 (Lic.).
Feb. 15, 1829.
Higgs, Lewis & Nancy F. Barbee, Jul 2, 1829 (Bond).
Hilary W. Barbee, BM.
Higgs, Lewis & Nancy F. Barbee, Jul. 2, 1836 (Lic.).
Jul. 6, 1836.
Hill, James & Amanda Williams, Dec. 30, 1833 (Bond).
John R. Halford, BM.
Hill, Lewis & Polly Lakey, Sep. 13, 1829 (Bond).
Norton Chisholm (Chism), BM.
Hill, Lewis & Polly Lakey, Sep. 13, 1829 (Lic.).
Sep. 14, 1829.
Hill, William W. & Lurainey Thompson, Jun. 23, 1825
(Lic.). Jun. 24, 1825.
Hinds, Jessy & Malinda Earwood, Jul. 31, 1837 (Lic.).
Aug. 1, 1837.
Hinsley, James & Elizabeth Weaver, Jun. 28, 1823 (Bond).
Nathan Bassham, BM.
Hinsley, James & Elizabeth Weaver, Jun. 28, 1823 (Lic.).
Jun. 29, 1823.
Hoge, Moses & Eliza Ann Napier, Apr. 9, 1837 (Bond).
Felix A. Catron, BM.
Holland, Basdale (Basil) & Elizabeth Fisher, Oct. 6, 1838
(Bond). William Eastes, BM.
Holland, Basdale (Basil) & Elizabeth Fisher, Oct. 6, 1828
(Lic.). Oct. 7, 1828.

Holland, Henry & Nancy Oldham, Dec. 6, 1838 (Lic.).
    Dec. 6, 1838.
Holland, William & Minerva Jane Miller, Mar. 16, 1836
    (Bond). William Moody Security, BM.
Hollis, Joseph & Isabella Wilie, Mar. 18, 1831 (Bond).
    Alexander Armstrong, BM.
Hollis, William & Sally Moore, Nov. 14, 1827 (Lic.).
    Nov. 18, 1827.
Hollis, William & Sally Moore, Nov. 18, 1827 (Lic.).
    Nov. 18, 1827.
Hollis, William & Sarah Kilburn, Nov. 6, 1837 (Lic.).
    Nov. 6, 1837.
Holloway, James & Nancy Day, Feb. 29, 1826 (Lic.).
    Jul. 30, 1826.
Holloway, Jesse & Polly Brashears, Jan. 3, 1829 (Bond).
    John Holloway, BM.
Holloway, Sidney & Milly Jones, Mar. 20, 1830 (Lic.).
    Mar. 21, 1830.
Holt, John & Sally Poteet, Feb. 5, 1831 (Bond).
    William R. Holt, BM.
Holt, John & Sally Poteet, Feb. 5, 1831 (Lic.).
    Feb. 6, 1831.
Holt, Thomas & Lear Shelton, Feb. 21, 1831 (Bond).
    Hezekiah Shelton, BM.
Horn, Grisham & Rebecca Poteet, Jan. 7, 1833 (Bond).
    Thomas Horn, BM.
Howard, Elsey & Margery Allen, Jan. 29, 1838 (Lic.).
    Jan. 30, 1838.
Howard, Thomas & Rosannah Comer, Sep. 2, 1835 (Bond).
    Jesse Belew, BM.
Hughs, David & Barbary Roberson, Sep. 6, 1832 (Lic.).
    Sep. 16, 1832.
Hughs, William & Mary Robertson, Nov. 20, 1821 (Bond).
    B. Halford, BM.
Hurst, William W. & Janey (?), Sep. 29, 1838 (Bond).
    Jacob H. Blasingame, BM.
Hutchenson, Tennesson & Elizabeth Peoples, Sep. 9, 1830
    (Bond). Miles Birdsong, BM.
Hutcherson, William & Laydia W. Morris, Jul. 31, 1837
    (Lic.). Aug. 2, 1837.

Irby, Henry & Pelina Brown, Feb. 14, 1838 (Bond).
    Isaac Gibson, BM.
Irby, Henry & Pelina Brown, Feb. 14, 1838 (Lic.).
    Feb. 15, 1838.

James, Andrew J. & Eliza Mason, Mar. 3, 1838 (Lic.).
    Mar. 3, 1838.
Jobe, John & Sally Farmer, Sep. 21, 1818 (Lic.).
    Sep. 21, 1818.
Jobe, Nathan & Martha Asbell, Feb. 27, 1821 (Lic.).
    Mar. 7, 1821.
Johnson, Aaron & Purgy Miller, Jun. 3, 1837 (Lic.).
    Jun. 4, 1837.

Johnson, Henry M. & Matilda Dunlap, Nov. 10, 1830
   (Bond). John A. Johnston, BM.
Johnston, William & Elizabeth Johnston, Jan. 17, 1823
   (Bond). Aaron Springer, BM.
Jones, James & Sally Wisdom, Nov. 8, 1828 (Bond).
   Thomas Wisdom, BM.
Jones, James & Sally Wisdom, Nov. 8, 1828 (Lic.).
   Nov. 8, 1828.
Jordan, Anderson & Darkis Millin, Jul. 27, 1831 (Bond).
   William Lockart, BM.
Jordan, Anderson & Darkis Millin, Jul. 27, 1831 (Lic.).
   Jul. 28, 1831.
Joyce, William & Susanna Webb, Jun. 8, 1837 (Bond).
   G.F. Napier, BM.

Keelam, Manville or Kellon, Maxville & Parmelia Altum,
   Dec. 9, 1835 (Bond). Jackson A. Altum, BM.
Keelan, Manville or Kellon, Maxville & Parmelia Altum,
   Dec. 9, 1835 (Lic.). Dec. 14, 1835.
Keelen, William & Katy Burnet, Aug. 31, 1826 (Lic.).
   Jul. 28, 1826.
Keeton, Zachariah & Katharine Anthony, Oct. 21, 1834
   (Lic.). Oct. 22, 1834.
Keeton, Zachariah & Katharine Anthony, Oct. 21, 1834
   (Bond). John Byrris, BM.
Kelly, James & Elizabeth Lindsey, Jul. 31, 1820 (Bond).
   Ellett Lindsey, BM.
Kelly, James & Jane Hail, --- 183_ (Bond). Elsy Howard, BM.
Kelly, John J. & Susannah M. Boswell, Dec. 1, 1835 (Bond).
   James Kelly, BM.
Kelly, John J. & Susannah M. Boswell, Dec. 1, 1835 (Lic.).
   Dec. 1, 1835.
Kelly, John M. & Susannah R. Taylor, Sep. 27, 1835 (Lic.).
   Sep. 28, 1835.
Kelly, John M. & Susannah R. Taylor, Sep. 27, 1835 (Bond).
   Thomas J. Matthews and C.J. Herrin, BM.
Kendrick, Obediah & Sarah Price, Mar. 18, 1825 (Bond).
   Hansford Tutt, BM.
Kendrick, Obediah & Sarah Price, Mar. 19, 1825 (Lic.).
   Mar. 23, 1825.
Kendrick, Thomas F.A. & Elanor C. Roland, Aug. 19, 1837
   (Bond). E.N. Lindsey, BM.
Kelly, John A. & Nancy Ann Horton, Dec. 7, 1830 (Bond).
   John G. McDonald, BM.
Kimbrell, Bassell & (?), Dec. 29, 1824 (Bond).
   Thomas Spencer, BM.
Kimbrell, Jesse & Nancy Gist, Jul. 20, 1820 (Bond).
   Thomas Spencer, BM.
Kimbrell, Jesse & Nancy Gist, Jul. 14, 1820 (Lic.).
   Jul. 17, 1820.
Kirksey, Jesse B. & Cinthy Kirk, Apr. 6, 1835 (Bond).
   Stephen Carrell, BM.
Kutch, Solomon & Lena Byrket, May 12, 1832 (Lic.).
   May 17, 1832.

LaCroix, Jacob & Mary Radford, Jul. 16, 1827 (Bond).
    Thos. J. Matthews, BM.
LaCroix, Jacob & Mary Radford, Jul. 16, 1827 (Lic.).
    Jul. 17, 1827.
Lancaster, Braddock & Ceneth Vandiver, Aug. 29, 1838
    (Lic.).
Lancaster, Nathaniel & Nancy Dial, Jan. 22, 1834 (Bond).
    James Chambers, BM.
Lancaster, Nathaniel & Nancy Dial, Jan. 22, 1834 (Lic.).
    Jan. 28, 1834.
Land, Benjamin & Beckey Jackson, Nov. 28, 1825 (Bond).
    Henry R. Davis, BM.
Lanier, Turner & Louisa Templeton, Apr. 14, 1838 (Lic.).
Layton, Felix I. & Mary Walker, Oct. 10, 1831 (Bond).
    Carroll Morris, BM.
Layton, Felix I. & Mary Walker, Oct. 10, 1831 (Lic.).
    Oct. 10, 1831.
Layton, John & Lavine Burket, Jun. 22, 1832 (Bond).
    Shadrack Morris, BM.
Leamons, Robert & Eady Yomans, Mar. 4, 1822 (Bond).
    David Pennington, BM.
Leamons, Robert & Eady Yomans, Mar. 4, 1822 (Lic.).
    Mar. 4, 1822.
Ledbetter, Wm. F. & Mary Craig, Jan. 8, 1838 (Bond).
    Adam Craig, BM.
Lee, James & Sally Spears, Sep. 6, 1835 (Bond).
    George Sanders, BM.
Leigh (Lee), William J. & Louisa Watson, Feb. 14, 1837
    (Bond). Nelson McMillin, BM.
Leigh (Lee), William J. & Louisa Watson, Feb. 14, 1837
    (Lic.). Feb. 14, 1837.
LeMay, Woodford N. & Nancy Bassham, Apr. 28, 1838 (Lic.).
    Apr. 28, 1838.
Lemmons, Craig & Sarah Brashears, Jul. 1, 1837 (Bond).
    John Carter, BM.
Lemmons, Craig & Sarah Brashears, Jul. 1, 1837 (Lic.).
    Jul. 2, 1837.
Lemmons, Silas & Mahaly Yeomans, Mar. 4, 1823 (Lic.).
    Apr. 7, 1823.
Lewis, Benjamin P. & Sarah McMasters, Nov. 19, 1831 (Bond).
    Johnathan White, BM.
Lewis, Benjamin P. & Sarah McMasters, Nov. 19, 1831 (Lic.).
    Nov. 19, 1831.
Lewis, Levi & Nancy Hemphill, Apr. 5, 1819 (Bond).
    Wilson Weaver, BM.
Lewis, John & Barbary Hencely, Jun. 11, 1836 (Lic.).
    Jun. 16, 1836.
Linam, Thomas J. & Sarah Ranolds, Oct. 18, 1837 (Bond).
    Charles W. Bowden, BM.
Lince, Isaac & Mary Arnold, Dec. 16, 1835 (Bond).
    Edward Arnold and A.J. Altum, BM.
Lindsey, Collum & Nancy Heldridge, Mar. 27, 1826 (Bond).
    Andrew Elison, BM.
Lindsey, Daniel & Elizabeth Wisdom, Apr. 25, 1821 (Bond).
    Starling Lindsey, BM.

LAWRENCE COUNTY MARRIAGES

Lindsey, Daniel & Elizabeth Wisdom, Apr. 25, 1821 (Lic.).
    Apr. 26, 1821.
Lindsey, Daniel & Sally Daulton, May 6, 1836 (Bond).
    Ezekiel Lindsey, BM.
Lindsey, Daniel & Sally Daulton, May 6, 1836 (Lic.).
    May 8, 1836.
Lindsey, E.N. & Solinah Bailey, Nov. 9, 1837 (Bond).
    Stephanis Busby, BM.
Lindsey, E.N. & Solinah Bailey, Nov. 9, 1837 (Lic.).
    Nov. 9, 1837.
Lindsey, Ezekiel & Mary Ann McCallister, May 14, 1829
    (Bond). Joseph L. Paine, BM.
Lindsey, Green L. & Elizabeth C. Crisp, Jun. 17, 1824
    (Lic.). Jun. 17, 1824.
Lindsey, Hillard & Mary Stone, Nov. 17, 1829 (Bond).
    John A. Reese, BM.
Lindsey, Jefferson & Nancy Wisdom, May 19, 1824 (Bond).
    Ezekiel Lindsey, BM.
Lintz, Wilson & Nancy Baker, Oct. 4, 1831 (Lic.).
    Oct. 6, 1831.
Lindsey, Joseph & Morning Hammons, Oct. 12, 1818 (Bond).
    James McFall, BM.
Loag, John & Mary Ann Brooks, Dec. 25, 1836 (Lic.).
    Dec. 22, 1836.(sic)
Lockard, Almon A. & Rachael Goforth, Sep. 2, 1828 (Bond).
    Richd. Massey, BM.
Lockard, Almon A. & Rachael Goforth, Sep. 2, 1828 (Lic.).
    Oct. 6, 1828.
Lockard, William & May Chronister, Apr. 20, 1822 (Bond).
    Wm. Winn, BM.
Locke, Rolin (Rowland) J. & Elizabeth Hare, Sep. 19, 1829
    (Bond). Moses Woodard, BM.
Long, William C. & Malinda Wallace, Oct. 13, 1818 (Bond).
    Eli Canaday, BM.
Lovve, Martin A. & Francis M. Forest, Aug. 2, 1837 (Bond).
    Newton C. Womack, BM.
Lovve, Martin A. & Francis M. Forest, Aug. 2, 1837 (Lic.).
    Aug. 2, 1827.
Lucas, John H. & Vilothy Matthews, Apr. 10, 1832 (Bond).
    Samuel M. Wasson, BM.
Lucas, Thomas & Susan Ingram, Sep. 9, 1834 (Bond).
    William Counts, BM.
Lumpkins, Jesse B. & Elizabeth Bryant, Mar. 19, 1836
    (Lic.). Mar. 13, 1836.
Lumpkins, William H. & Eliza Smith, Feb. 10, 1836 (Bond).
    Mel. Lanier, BM.
Lumpkins, William H. & Eliza Smith, Feb. 10, 1836
    (Lic.). Feb. 11, 1838.
Lynes, George & Ann Flournoy, Oct. 12, 1818 (Bond).
    Warrer Mason, BM.
Lyons, Pilate & Mahaly Farmer, Jan. 23, 1834 (Bond).
    Solomon Miles, BM.
Lyons, Pilate & Mahaly Farmer, Jan. 23, 1834 (Lic.).
    Jan. 23, 1834.

LAWRENCE COUNTY MARRIAGES

Lyons, Pilate & Rebecca Davis, Jun. 18, 1835 (Bond).
William Ethridge, BM.
Manas, (?) & Sarah Arnold, Sep. 22, 1836 (Bond).
Edward Arnold, BM.
Manuel, Paton & -nny Adams, Jan. 12, 1822 (Lic.).
Feb. 22, 1822.
Manuel, Phillip & Sarah Fondren, Nov. 24, 1836 (Lic.).
Nov. 26, 1834. (sic)
Marcum, Lewis & Peggy Senter, Jan. 5, 1830 (Lic.).
Jan. 21, 1830.
Mason, Wm. R. & Lucinda Burris, Dec. 10, 1835 (Bond).
David L. Duncan, BM.
Mason, Wm. R. & Lucinda Burris, Dec. 10, 1835 (Lic.).
Dec. 10, 1835.
Massey, Richard A. & Lavina Herralston, Aug. 6, 1828
(Bond). Stephen Carrell, BM.
Matlock, William & Joycey Waldrip, Apr. 4, 1835 (Bond).
John Sapplington, BM.
Matthews, Jacob & Virginia Bell, Jan. 28, 1833 (Bond).
Henry Sharp, BM.
Matthews, Lewis & Ruthy Billingsley, Aug. 13, 1818
(Lic.). Aug. 13, 1818.
Matthews, Thomas J. & Catharine Beeler, Aug. 10, 1830
(Bond). Calvin McCrackin, BM.
Maxey, Edward & Polly Nelson, Jan. 14, 1821 (Lic.).
Jan. 14, 1821.
Maxey, William M. & Sarah Nelson, Feb. 4, 1826 (Bond).
John Nelson, BM.
Maxey, William M. & Sarah Nelson, Feb. 4, 1826 (Lic.).
Feb. 5, 1826.
May, Frederick & Lovice Right, Sep. 19, 1833 (Lic.).
Sep. 19, 1833.
May, Moses & Pattsey Rackley, Jan. 12, 1828 (Lic.).
Jan. 13, 1828.
May, William & Mary Brashears, Mar. 23, 1825 (Bond).
Henry Brashears, BM.
Melton, Elisha & Clarasey Rogers, Apr. 6, 1825 (Bond).
Elijah Melton, BM.
Melton, William & Catharine McIntire, Jul. 30, 1825
(Bond). Joshua Bowdry, BM.
Merchant, John & Sally Walker, Feb. 22, 1821 (Lic.).
Mar. 31, 1821.
Merchant, Richard & Prudy Waldrip, Oct. 11, 1825 (Bond).
Thos. J. Matthews, BM.
Middleton, John W. & Sally Inman, Oct. 15, 1822 (Bond).
Peter P. Alsup, BM.
Miles, Sebourn & Nancy Waldrip, Aug. 1, 1835 (Bond).
Thomas Cook, BM.
Miles, Sebourn & Nancy Waldrip, Aug. 1, 1835 (Lic.).
Aug. 6, 1835.
Miller, Joseph & Eliza C. Lucus, Jun. 20, 1836 (Lic.).
Jun. 21, 1836.

Mitchell, Thomas & Lisey Waters, Feb. 3, 1825 (Bond).
  Jesse Hutcheson, BM.
Mitchell, Thomas & Lisey Waters, Feb. 3, 1825 (Lic.).
  Feb. 1825.
Monday, John & Barbary Allen, Mar. 28, 1832 (Lic.).
  Mar. 29, 1832.
Moody, Isaac & Sabra Moody, Jan. 11, 1836 (Bond).
  James Hensley, BM.
Moody, James & Lucinda Hensley, Apr. 30, 1831 (Bond).
  William Moody, BM.
Moody, Jonathan & Sarah Randall, Aug. 23, 1836 (Bond).
  William Moody, BM.
Moody, Jonathan & Sarah Randall, Aug. 23, 1836 (Lic.).
  Aug. 24, 1836.
Moody, John & Martha Perrimon, Aug. 14, 1837 (Bond).
  Joseph Sanders, BM.
Moody, Parker & Sally Holloway, Jul. 5, 1828 (Bond).
  William Moody, BM.
Moore, William & Marinda Thornton, Jan. 4, 1825 (Bond).
  William Melton, BM.
Morgan, Jonathan & Jane Venable, Oct. 13, 1819 (Bond).
  Nathan McClendon, BM.
Morris, Eli & Sibbey Spears, Nov. 21, 1825 (Bond).
  William Morris, BM.
Morris, Isaac & Rebecca Davis, Aug. 27, 1838 (Bond).
  Brad Lancaster, BM.
Morris, Isaac & Rebecca Davis, Aug. 27, 1838 (Lic.).
  Aug. 27, 1838.
Morris, Gresham & Sarah Martin, May 20, 1832 (Bond).
  W.P.A. McCabe, BM.
Morris, John & Jane Altum, Mar. 13, 1832 (Lic.).
  Mar. 15, 1832.
Morrow, Thomas & Mary Wilie, Dec. 17, 1831 (Lic.).
  Dec. 18, 1831.
Musgrove, Bennett & (?) Robertson, Nov. 20, 1821 (Bond).
  Annul Keltner, BM.
Musgrave, Jonas & Rebecah Tracet, Jul. 1, 1819 (Lic.).
Myers, George & Anney Burke, Oct. 6, 1828 (Bond).
  William Quillen, BM.
Myers, George & Anney Burke, Oct. 6, 1828 (Lic.).
  Oct. 16, 1828.
Myers, George & Sally Coker, May 15, 1832 (Lic.).
Myers, Perry & Cinthy Cooper, Nov. 26, 1825 (Bond).
  John Fisher, BM.
Myres, Perry & Charlotte Markham, May 4, 1833 (Lic.).
  May 5, 1833.

McAnally, Charles & Elizabeth Simpson, Nov. 27, 1823
  (Bond). G.W. Hanks, BM.
McAnally, Charles & Elizabeth Simpton, Nov. 23, 1823
  (Lic.). Dec. 8, 1823.
McAnally, Elisha & (?), Dec. 29, 1824 (Bond).
  Wm. Clark, BM.

LAWRENCE COUNTY MARRIAGES

McCannally, Martin & Pearcy Sharp, Dec. 21, 1825 (Bond).
    Charles Herrin, BM.
McCafferty, William & Nancy Springer, Jan. 21, 1824 (Bond).
    Aaron Springer, BM.
McCafferty, William & Nancy Springer, Jan. 21, 1824 (Lic.).
    Jan. 22, 1824.
McCann, Arthur & Ann Futrell, Jul. 23, 1834 (Bond).
    William Cook, BM.
McCann, John & Polly Brashears, Sep. 24, 1833 (Bond).
    Starkey Sharp, BM.
McCain, William & Susanna Courtney, Nov. 13, 1819 (Bond).
    Hugh McCain, BM.
McClaren, Andrew & Leaner Johnson, Dec. 1818 (Bond).
    Robert Johnson, BM.
McClaren, Robert & Huldy Coker, Feb. 11, 1831 (Bond).
    G.F. Simonton, BM.
McClendon, Nathan & Caroline E. Franks, Dec. 1, 1832
    (Lic.). Dec. 6, 1832.
McConnell, Washington M. & Matilda Edmiston, Mar. 4, 1834
    (Lic.). Mar. 4, 1832.
McConnell, William & Nancy Garret, Oct. 10, 1822 (Lic.).
    Oct. 10, 1822.
McCormich, Washington & Matilda Edmiston, Mar. 4, 1834
    (Bond). Alexander Lee, BM.
McCoy, Samuel & Faithy Rodes, Aug. 30, 1834 (Bond).
    John Fondren, BM.
McDonald, Alexander & Sarah Howard, Aug. 24, 1818 (Lic.).
    Sep. 27, 1818.
McDougal, Daniel & Jane M. Holland, Oct. 7, 1838 (Bond).
    D.N. Cayce, BM.
McDougal, Daniel & Jane M. Holland, Oct. 7, 1838 (Lic.).
    Oct. 18, 1838.
McFalls, James & Parient Downs, Apr. 5, 1822 (Lic.).
    Apr. 9, 1822.
McGee, John & Sarah Tracy, May 19, 1832 (Lic.). May 20, 1832.
McGee, Joseph & Delia Culbreth, Feb. 26, 1823 (Bond).
    Daniel Culbreth, BM.
McGee, Micajah & Elizabeth Kilburn, Jun. 9, 1820 (Bond).
    James Burns, BM.
McHughs, Charles & Polly Roaland, Nov. 17, 1818 (Lic.).
McKey, Charles & Susan Cothen, Mar. 14, 1832 (Bond).
    James Cothen, BM.
McKnight, William & Louisa McCracken, Jun. 29, 1830
    (Lic.). Jun. 29, 1830.
McKnight, William, Jr. & Elvira D. Parks, Dec. 29, 1836
    (Bond). Stephanis Busby, BM.
McKnight, William, Jr. & Elvira D. Parks, Dec. 29, 1836
    (Lic.). Dec. 29, 1836.
McLain, John Biller & Eleanor Nipper, Jan. 8, 1838 (Bond).
    Clark Smith, BM.
McLaren, James & Cyntha Tays, Mar. 3, 1838 (Bond).
    Joe McIntyre, BM.
McLaren, James & Cyntha Tays, Mar. 3, 1838 (Lic.).
    Mar. 5, 1838.

21

McLaren, R.H. & Ann Pearce, May 26, 1837 (Bond).
Wm. R. Walker, BM.
McLaren, R.H. & Ann Pearce, May 26, 1837 (Lic.).
May 27, 1837.
McLean, Charles & Mary S. Duncan, Aug. 4, 1824 (Bond).
Isaac Rainey, BM.
McLean, Samuel D. & Elizabeth C. Wasson, Nov. 14, 1831
(Bond), Franklin Buchanan, BM.
McLean, Robert I. & Mary A.N. (Nancy) Shackelford,
Mar. 15, 1830 (Bond). William McKnight, Jr., BM.
McLean, Robert I. & Mary A.N. (Nancy) Shackelford,
Mar. 15, 1830 (Lic.). Mar. 16, 1830.
McMasters, Dan & Barshena Snodgrass, Jun. 27, 1838 (Lic.).
Jun. 27, 1838.
McMasters, Danieo & Lucinda Garner, Sep. 23, 1835 (Bond).
David L. Moore, BM.

Nail, Archer & Rebecca Morrow, Sep. 18, 1819 (Bond).
Douglas H. Stockton, BM.
Nail, Archer & Rebecca Morrow, Sep. 18, 1819 (Lic.).
Sep. 23, 1819.
Needham, Jesse & Aurey Edleman, Jul. 7, 1819 (Bond).
Daniel Pearce, BM.
Needham, John W. & Nancy Tucker, May 15, 1821 (Lic.).
Newburn, Eli & Hetty Shackelford, Aug. 29, 1838 (Lic.).
Newton, Smith & Elizabeth H. Johnston, Nov. 30, 1827
(Bond). D.H. Stockton, BM.
Newton, Smith & Elizabeth H. Johnston, Nov. 30, 1827
(Lic.). Dec. 3, 1827.
Newton, Thomas W. & Lucinda Powell, Jan. 6, 1835 (Bond).
William E. Newton, BM.
Nipper, Isaac & Spicy Scales, Nov. 7, 1837 (Bond).
Elijah W. Keese, BM.
Norman, Lewis & Elizabeth Ann Morris, Mar. 5, 1838 (Lic.).
Mar. 5, 1838.
Norman, Thomas W. & Cyreney Clifton, Jan. 5, 1837 (Bond).
Levi Welch, BM.
Norman, Thomas W. & Cyreney Clifton, Jan. 5, 1837 (Lic.).
Jan. 5, 1837.
Norman, Wilson B. & Lavina J. Wasson, Jan. 15, 1833
(Lic.). Jan. 15, 1833.
Null, Isaac & Sally Askew, Aug. 11, 1825 (Bond).
Micager Baker, BM.
Normines, Geophrey & Amy Normines, Apr. 27, 1828 (Bond).
William Henry, BM.
Nunn, Francis & Mary G. McWhirter, Jan. 9, 1830 (Bond).
John F. McWhirter, BM.

Pace, Thomas & Mary Hendrix, July 17, 1823 (Bond).
Herton Hamilton, BM.
Pace, Thomas & Mary Hendrix, July 17, 1823 (Lic.)
July 18, 1823.
Paine, William & Jane J. Hardin, Jan. 26, 1834 (Bond).
Josiah Tatum.

LAWRENCE COUNTY MARRIAGES

Palmore, Claborn & Lucinda Peoteet, Jan. 2, 1830 (Bond).
   Samuel Ellison, BM.
Parchman, James & Sally Welch, Apr. 4, 1818 (Lic.).
   Apr. 9, 1818.
Parker, William & Elizabeth Stribling, Jan. 19, 1836
   (Bond). J.M. Bumpass, BM.
Parks, Dudley J. & Nancy A. Cayce, Jan. 8, 1837 (Bond).
   Stephanis Busby, BM.
Parks, Willie S. & Benety Ann Hight, May 28, 1830
   (Bond). B. Halford, BM.
Parks, Willie S. & Benety Ann Hight, May 28, 1830 (Lic.).
   May 30, 1830.
Parnell, John B. & Jane Sharp, Nov. 4, 1824 (Bond).
   Richard B. Tutt, BM.
Parrett, James & Margaret Centee, Apr. 15, 1829 (Lic.).
   July 6, 1829.
Pate, Thomas & Elizabeth Burman, Jan. 29, 1824 (Bond).
   Joseph Thomas, BM.
Pearce, Jesse & Caroline Pearce, Sept. 23, 1830 (Bond).
   Jacob Bird, BM.
Pearce, Joseph & Lucy D. Flood, Apr. 4, 1825 (Bond).
   George Michie, BM.
Pearc, Robert & Fanny Wester, Oct. 8, 1824 (Bond).
   H. Day, BM.
Pennington, Jacob & Numinty Armstrong, Feb. 13, 1829
   (Lic.). Feb. 23, 1829.
Pennington, John W. & Patience Tutts, Dec. 18, 1836
   (Bond). Leroy Pennington, BM.
Peoples, Rubin & Mary Hambrick, Dec. 30, 1820 (Bond).
   Solomon Gresham, BM.
Peoples, Rubin & Mary Hambrick, Dec. 29, 1820 (Lic.).
   Jan. 3, 1821.
Perkins, Andrew M. & Letty Voss, Aug. 11, 1832 (Bond).
   Stephan Matthews, BM.
Perkins, Andrew M. & Letty Voss, Aug. 11, 1832 (Lic.).
   Aug. 14, 1832.
Perkins, John & Nancy Anthony, Sept. 26, 1831 (Bond).
   Stephen Matthews, BM.
Perrymore, Matthew & Lucy B. Warren, July 2, 1836
   (Lic.). July 3, 1836.
Petty, Joshua & Patsy Price, Aug. 4, 1830 (Bond).
   John Price, BM.
Peyton, Jesse H. & Malinda Calhoon, Sept. 4, 1830
   (Bond). Thos. J. Matthews, BM.
Pickard, William & Malinda Gibson, May 22, 1833 (Bond).
   Thomas Baker, BM.
Pickard, William & Malinda Gibson, May 22, 1833 (Lic.).
   May 25, 1833.
Pickens, Israel L. & Sally Rutledge, Sept. 25, 1818
   (Bond). Robert Johnson, BM.
Pierce, John & Rebecca Bradley, Sept. 16, 1831 (Lic.).
   Sept. 26, 1831.
Pipen, Kinchen & Jane Brashears, Nov. 9, 1836 (Lic.).
   Nov. 14, 1836.

23

Pippins, John & Letitia Walke, Jan. 14, 1836 (Bond).
Francis Walker, BM.
Pippins, Richard & Nelly Brashears, Apr. 26, 1825 (Bond).
Harden Payne, BM.
Pippins, Simeon & Rachael Cole, Nov. 11, 1825 (Lic.).
Nov. 12, 1835.
Pollock, Daniel & Rhody Christian, Oct. 9, 1827 (Bond).
Isham Christian, BM.
Pollock, David & Mary McElyeo, Feb. 10, 1830 (Bond).
William Pollock and Samuel McElyeo, BM.
Pollock, Elisha & Martha Christian, Feb. 6, 1828 (Bond).
James C. Nichols, BM.
Pollock, Elisha & Martha Christian, Feb. 6, 1828 (Lic.).
Feb. 7, 1828.
Pollock, James & Nancy Hightower, July 4, 1822 (Lic.).
July 13, 1822.
Pollock, Samuel J. & Carolina H. Murphy, Aug. 4, 1837
(Bond). Wm. R. Walker, BM.
Pool, Sanders & Sophia Duckworth, Jan. 27, 1820 (Lic.).
Feb. 3, 1820.
Pope, John & Rebecca Looters, July 25, 1827 (Bond).
John Ramsey, BM.
Pope, John & Rebecca Looters, July 25, 1827 (Lic.).
July 26, 1827.
Porter, John & Malinda Bassham, Dec. 27, 1837 (Bond).
John Miller, BM.
Poteet, Isaac & Barbary McLemore, Jan. 29, 1824 (Bond).
Samuel D. Poteet, BM.
Poteet, Samuel D. & Margaret Snodgrass, Apr. 2, 1836
(Lic.). Apr. 5, 1836.
Powell, Gilford & Elizabeth Trip, June 10, 1826 (Lic.).
June 10, 1826.
Powell, Joshua W. & Tebitha P. Hogg, Feb. 18, 1825
(Bond). Robert Hogg, BM.
Powell, Joshua & Tebitha P. Hogg, Feb. 18, 1825 (Lic.).
Feb. 18, 1825.
Pratt, James,& Eleanor Stewart, Dec. 14, 1832. (Bond).
William Davis, BM.
Prewitt, Patrick H. & Mary Morrow, Dec. 21, 1825 (Lic.).
Dec. 22, 1825.
Price, Daniel & Emily Burns, Jan. 28, 1834 (Bond).
Israel Burns, BM.
Price, Ezekiel & Martha Williams, Jan. 25, 1830 (Bond).
John Price, BM.
Prince, David & Hannah Stewart, Mar. 21, 1833 (Bond).
William Millstead, BM.
Pullen, Isham & Unita Ann Pearce, Dec. 9, 1835 (Bond).
John Mason, BM.

Rackley, Hyram & Sarah LeMay, Jan. 16, 1838 (Bond).
Wm. J.W. Moore, BM.
Rackley, Hyram & Sarah LeMay, Jan. 16, 1836 (Lic.).
Jan. 16, 1836.
Rackley, Josiah W. & Eliza Brown, Sept. 12, 1838 (Bond).
Wm. Rackley, BM.

Rackley, Josiah W. & Eliza Brown, Sept. 12, 1838 (Lic.).
    Sept. 12, 1838.
Rackley, Passons & Franky Melton, Dec. 18, 1821 (Lic.).
    Dec. 21, 1821.
Rackley, Purvis & Sally Bell, Sept. 1, 1829 (Lic.).
    Sept. 1, 1829.
Radford, John C. & Mary Clifton, June 10, 1837 (Lic.).
    June 13, 1837.
Rainey, Isaac & Elizabeth H. Pryer, Dec. 21, 1824 (Bond).
    R.J. Hill, BM.
Ramsey, Joel & Susannah Terrell, July 13, 1837 (Bond).
    Lewis Dalton, BM.
Ramsey, Joel & Susannah Terrell, July 13, 1837 (Lic.).
    July 13, 1837.
Ramsey, Richard & Zilphy Christian, May 30, 1822 (Bond).
    R.T. Bailey, BM.
Randall, Benjamin & Darcus Moody, Mar. 9, 1836 (Bond).
    Joseph Sanders, BM.
Randall, Benjamin & Dorcas Moody, Mar. 9, 1836 (Lic.).
    Mar. 10, 1836.
Randall, Thomas & Elizabeth Hide, Feb. 12, 1838 (Bond).
    William Cates, BM.
Randall, Thomas & Elizabeth Hide, Feb. 12, 1838 (Lic.).
    Feb. 12, 1838.
Ratliff, David & Malinda Voss, Dec. 29, 1829 (Bond).
    John Voss, BM.
Ratliff, David & Malinda Voss, Dec. 29, 1829 (Lic.).
    Dec. 31, 1829.
Reed, Henry N. & Susan Tucker, Oct. 5, 1837 (Bond).
    Thomas J. Waggoner, BM.
Reeder, Thomas J. & Ealinor Campbell, Jan. 19, 1824
    (Bond). William W. Beeler, BM.
Reeves, Redding & Jane Burkett, Sept. 1, 1829 (Bond).
    Thomas Baker, BM.
Reeves, Redding & Jane Burkett, Sept. 1, 1829 (Lic.).
    Sept. 3, 1829.
Renfroe, Levi & Elizabeth Pickard, Aug. 22, 1835 (Bond).
    George F. Sharp, BM.
Renfroe, Levi & Elizabeth Pickard, Aug. 22, 1835 (Lic.).
    Aug. 25, 1825.
Renfro, William & Lucreska Johnson, Apr. 12, 1837
    (Bond). Pasons Rackley, BM.
Renfro, William & Lucreska Johnson, Apr. 12, 1837
    (Lic.). Apr. 12, 1837.
Reynolds, Gilliard Brice & Sally Reynolds, Dec. 24, 1824
    (Bond). William Reynolds, BM.
Rhodes (Roads?), Hamilton & Synthia Smith, Nov. 19, 1835
    (Bond). John Fondren, BM.
Rhodes (Roads), Hamilton & Synthia Smith, Nov. 19, 1835
    (Lic.). Nov. 19, 1835.
Richardson, John P. & Anna May, June 30, 1838 (Lic.).
    July 3, 1838.
Richardson, Thomas A. & Harriet Wisdom, Dec. 1, 1835
    (Lic.). Dec. 1, 1835.

Richardson, Thomas A. & Lucy C. Burkit, Apr. 23, 1838
  (Bond). Sam Dickson, BM.
Richardson, Thomas A. & Lucy C. Burkit, Apr. 23, 1838
  (Lic.). Apr. 24, 1838.
Right, Lorenzo D. & Lucinda Hill, May 12, 1831 (Bond).
  Tilman B. Parks, BM.
Roberson, John & Polly Blythe, May 23, 1836 (Lic.).
  May 24, 1836.
Roberts, Hyram & Sally Helton, Dec. 28, 1836 (Lic.).
  Dec. 29, 1836.
Roberts, Rial & Matilda Burris, Apr. 3, 1834 (Bond).
  Richard Burris, BM.
Roberts, Thomas & Elmira Gilbert, Apr. 3, 1834 (Bond).
  Rial J. Roberts, BM.
Roberts, Thos. J. & Leticia Beatty, Jun. 19, 1826 (Bond).
  W.A. Williams, BM.
Roberts, Thomas J. & Martha Doyal, Mar. 23, 1838 (Lic.).
  Mar. 26, 1838.
Robertson, James & Amy Tracy, Nov. 25, 1826 (Bond).
  Wilson Hillhouse, BM.
Robertson, James M. & Jane Brashears, Mar. 23, 1836
  (Bond). Thomas Robertson, BM.
Robertson, Miles & Olive Cohorn, Aug. 28, 1827 (Bond).
  George Hartwick, BM.
Robertson, Tyree & Dicey Moore, Oct. 1, 1833 (Bond).
  Thomas Choat, BM.
Robinson, James & Mirning Vatters, Sep. 29, 1826 (Bond).
  Alagany Vatters, BM.
Robinson, Joseph & Cynthy Votters, Jun. 8, 1824 (Bond).
  Bracewell Farmer, BM.
Robinson, Joseph & Margaret Parrett, Jan. 8, 1838 (Bond).
  Lewis Markham, BM.
Robinson, Joseph & Margaret Parrett, Jan. 8, 1838 (Lic.).
  Jan. 8, 1838.
Rogers, Berry H. & Matilda R.M. Wimpy, Jun. 11, 1831
  (Bond). Daniel W. McIntyre, BM.
Rogers, Berry H. & Matilda R.M. Wimpy, Jun. 11, 1831
  (Lic.). Jun. 13, 1831.
Rogers, Gimri & Any Davis, May 27, 1837 (Bond).
  Stephen L. Davis, BM.
Rogers, Williamson & Vina Cook, Aug. 1, 1832 (Bond).
  Plate Lyons, BM.
Rogers, Williamson & Vina Cook, Aug. 1, 1832 (Lic.).
  Aug. 1, 1832.
Roland, Stephen & Sally McKew, Oct. 12, 1818 (Bond).
  Charles McKew, BM.
Romines, Nocholas & Libey Spears, Jul. 7, 1829 (Bond).
  Sandford Bramlett, BM.
Rose, Mark M. & Hannah McCann, Sep. 11, 1837 (Bond).
  Jesse Sanders, BM.
Rose, Mark M. & Hannah McCann, Sep. 11, 1837 (Lic.).
Rountree, C.B. & Leucinda C. Sessums, Feb. 28, 1822
  (Lic.). Feb. 28, 1822.

Rowan, James J. & Matilda Holland, May 18, 1837 (Bond).
Thomas Pace, BM.
Sanders, Benjamin & Polly Moody, Jan. 8, 1834 (Bond).
Joseph Sanders, BM.
Sanders, Elijah & Elizabeth Noblitt, Oct. 4, 1824 (Bond).
W.L. Turner, BM.
Sanders, Jacob & Hannah A. Morton, Oct. 29, 1834 (Bond).
Joseph Sanders, BM.
Sanders, Joseph & Catharine Moody, May 7, 1829 (Bond).
James M. Ross, BM.
Sanders, Joseph & Catharine Moody, May 7, 1829 (Lic.).
May 7, 1829.
Sandy, Henry & Shu Hursaid Right, Nov. 21, 1831?(Bond).
Samuel D. Poteet, BM.
Sandy, Henry & Shu Hursaid Right, Nov. 21, 1821 (Lic.).
Nov. 25, 1821.
Scags, William & Susannah Brashears, Feb. 14, 1828
(Bond). Alexander Brashears, BM.
Scales, Richard H. & Joannah Mack, Sept. 14, 1837
(Bond). James Fondren, BM.
Scales, Richard & Joannah Mack, Sept. 14, 1837 (Lic.).
Dec. 17, 1837.
Scott, Franklin & Betsy Tennyson, Nov. 9, 1837 (Bond).
Hasten Spears, BM.
Seaton, John & Sally Hail, May 7, 1823 (Bond).
James E. Hail.
Sharp, Basil & H.R.B. Choat, July 1, 1829 (Lic.).
July 6, 1829.
Sharp, Starkey & America Harrison, July 13, 1836 (Lic.).
July 14, 1836.
Shelton, Hezekiah & Polly Howard, Dec. 26, 1831 (Bond).
Elisha Cox, BM.
Shelton, Hezekiah & Polly Howard, Dec. 26, 1831 (Lic.).
Dec. 28, 1831.
Shelton, Stephen & Susan Carter, June 19, 1834 (Bond).
Elisha Cox, BM.
Shelton, Stephen & Susan Carter, June 19, 1834 (Lic.).
June 19, 1834.
Shields, John & Mary Miller, June 6, 1836 (Lic.).
June 13, 1836.
Shockley, Ephraim & Sarah Harlow, Aug. 4, 1835 (Bond).
Jacob Brashears, BM.
Shockley, Ephraim & Sarah Harlow, Aug. 4, 1835 (Lic.).
Aug. 5, 1835.
Signan, Abraham & Sakky Stroud, Sept. 19, 1818 (Bond).
James Brooks, BM.
Simonton, G.F. & Evelina Buchanan, July 14, 1829 (Bond).
John G. McDonald, BM.
Simonton, G.F. & Evelina Buchanan, July 14, 1829 (Lic.).
July 14, 1829.
Sima, William & Elizabeth Hutcheson, July 25, 1825 (Bond).
William Brumley, BM.
Sima, William & Elizabeth Harris, July 25, 1832 (Bond).
John Brumley, BM.

Sizemore, William & Milly Farmer, Nov. 12, 1820 (Bond).
Nathan Bassham, BM.
Smart, Sion & Jane Choat, Sept. 21, 1830 (Bond).
Ephraim Gresham, BM.
Smith, Allen & Serenah Chapman, Aug. 1, 1836 (Bond).
George W. Smith, BM.
Smith, Benjamin & Mary Williams, Dec. 16, 1830 (Bond).
Benjamin Williams, BM.
Smith, Caprell & Martha E. Franks, Dec. 1, 1836 (Bond).
George W. Franks, BM.
Smith, Furdinan & Ann Burliston, Jan. 23, 1837?(Bond).
Albert Brumley, BM.
Smith, Furdinan & Ann Burliston, Jan. 23, 1827 (Lic.).
Jan. 23, 1827.
Smith, George & Susan Tucker, May 15, 1830 (Bond).
Solomon W.C. Cunningham, BM.
Smith, George & Susan Tucker, May 15, 1830 (Lic.).
May 16, 1839. (sic)
Smith, John & Rebecca Reed, Mar. 12, 1819 (Bond).
John Shirley, BM.
Smith, John W. & Catharine Childress, Mar. 13, 1838
(Lic.). Mar. 14, 1838.
Spears, Joseph & Susan Childress, July 2, 1831 (Bond).
Hasten Spears, BM.
Springs, Jacob & Malinda C. Todd, Dec. 4, 1830 (Bond).
Willis Hammonds, BM.
Springer, John & Elizabeth Gaines, Dec. 20, 1831 (Bond).
Wm. Springer, BM.
Springer, John & Lucretia Powel, Mar. 4, 1833 (Lic.).
Mar. 7, 1833.
Springer, John W. & Sarah Comer, Dec. 22, 1832 (Lic.).
Dec. 23, 1832.
Springer, Jonas & Anny Brashears, Feb. 18, 1833 (Bond).
Archibald Morrow, BM.
Springer, Jonas & Anny Brashears, Feb. 18, 1933 (Lic.).
Feb. 18, 1833.
Springer, Thomas & Susannah Allsup, Jan. 19, 1820 (Bond).
James Springer, BM.
Springer, Uriah & Ruthey Belew, July 3, 1824 (Bond).
Jacob Belew, BM.
Staggs, Abram & Nancy Coalter, Sept. 30, 1832 (Lic.).
Sept. 30, 1832.
Step, James & Elizabeth Dunlap, Jan. 3, 1835 (Lic.).
Jan. , 1825.
Stewart, Alexander & Nancy McIntire, Dec. 25, 1823
(Bond). Alexander Campbell, BM.
Stewart, Alexander & Nancy McIntire, Dec. 25, 1823
(Lic.). Jan. 1, 1824.
Stewart, Joshua & Elizabeth Griffin, Jan. 6, 1829
(Bond). Berryman Burns, BM.
Stockton, Douglas H. & Emily Bumpass, Sept. 18, 1819
(Bond). Archer Nail, BM.
Stockton, Douglas H. & Emily Bumpass, Sept. 18, 1819
(Lic.). Sept. 25, 1819.

Stockton, Josiah S. & Elizabeth Welch, July 6, 1830
(Bond). Franklin, BM.
Stout, William M. & May Hindsley, Nov. 12, 1836 (Bond).
R.I. McLean, BM.
Stribling, Andrew H. & Sarah M. Elton, Jan. 5, 1837
(Bond). Samuel Mason, BM.
Stribling, Andrew H. & Sarah M. Elton, Jan. 5, 1837
(Lic.). Jan. 5, 1837.
Stribling, J.B. & Sophia Bumpass, Feb. 9, 1824 (Bond).
A.W. Bumpass, BM.
Strickland, Archibald & Margaret Foster, Apr. 3, 1823
(Bond). John Ashmore, BM.
Strickland, Jacob & Sarah Ann Hill, June 11, 1835 (Bond).
Jacobs Watters, BM.
Strickland, James C. & Margaret A. Craig, Aug. 29, 1833
(Lic.). Aug. 29, 1833.
Strickland, John E. & Cinthy Robertson, Mar. 11, 1825
(Bond). Joel Warren, BM.
Strickland, John E. & Cinthy Robertson, Apr. 11, 1825
(Lic.). Apr. 11, 1825.
Strickland, John G. & Gracy Campbell, Sept. 10, 1822
(Bond). Alexander Campbell, BM.
Strickland, John G. & Gracy Campbell, Sept. 12, 1822
(Lic.). Sept. 12, 1822.
Strickland, Norman W. & Sarah Vincent, Jan. 4, 1837
(Bond). John Burris, BM.
Sullivant, John R. & Martha Sullivant, Dec. 30, 1834
(Lic.). Dec. 30, 1834.
Sullivan, Jordan & Priscilla Campbell, Sept. 23, 1826
(Bond). Jesse Sullivan, BM.
Sullivan, Jordan & Priscilla Campbell, Sept. 23, 1826
(Lic.). Sept. 26, 1826.
Sulivant, Jordan & Sarah M. Welch, Mar. 14, 1835 (Bond).
John J. Bell, BM.
Sulivant, Jordan & Sarah M. Welch, Mar. 14, 1835 (Lic.).
Mar. 14, 1835.
Sullivant, Samuel W. & Polly Osburn, Feb. 9, 1819
(Bond). John McCann, BM.
Sweaney, Levi W. & Miry E. Blackard, Oct. 6, 1835 (Bond).
John J. Kelley, BM.
Sweaney, Levi W. & Miry E. Blackard, Oct. 4, 1835 (Lic.).
Oct. 4, 1835.
Swinney, William & Elizabeth Stewart, June 21, 1838
(Bond). Ephraim B. Green, BM.
Swinney, William & Elizabeth Stewart, June 21, 1838
(Lic.). July 2, 1838.
Syclesworth, William & Nancy Null, Aug. 11, 1829 (Bond).
Lewis Hill, BM.
Syclesworth, William & Nancy Null, Aug. 11, 1829 (Lic.).
Aug. 12, 1829.

Tanner, John & Cely Odam, Apr. 24, 1826 (Bond).
Burrell Brumley, BM.

Tennuson, William M. & Mary J. Wasson, Oct. 30, 1832
(Bond). J. Benjamin Tennisson, BM.
Terry, Jesse & Elizabeth Lindsey, Apr. 21, 1825 (Bond).
James Kelly, BM.
Terry, Moses & Elizabeth Cowen, July 29, 1824 (Bond).
Elliott Lindsey, BM.
Thomas, Ethelred & Catherine Gresham, Mar. 1, 1819
(Bond). Solomon Gresham, BM.
Thomas, Joseph & Mary Lindsey, Jan. 28, 1826 (Bond).
Thomas Pate, BM.
Thomason, John & Lucy Flood, Mar. 9, 1819 (Bond).
Wm. Michie, BM.
Thompson, John & Rebecca Trip, Jan. 23, 1822 (Bond).
Thomas Holland, BM.
Thornton, Sparling & Mary Johnston, Feb. 23, 1838
(Bond). Rial J. Roberts, BM.
Thornton, Sparling & Mary Johnston, Feb. 23, 1838
(Lic.).
Thornton, Thomas & Levinah Tracy, Oct. 25, 1834 (Bond).
Samuel Moore, BM.
Thornton, Thomas & Levinah Tracy, Oct. 25, 1834 (Lic.).
Jan. 5, 1835.
Tidwell, Abram C. & Sirena C. Majors, Dec. 23, 1833
(Lic.). Dec. 24, 1833.
Tracy, Tanahill & Kisire (Kosiah) Lindsey, Mar. 23, 1830
(Bond). James Kelly, BM.
Tredaway, John & Betsey Bradley, Oct. 1, 1831 (Bond).
Lewis Reddy, BM.
Treadway, John & Izeller Greenwood, Feb. 13, 1835 (Bond).
B.H. Rogers, BM.
Treadway, John & Izeller Greenwood, Feb. 13, 1835 (Lic.).
Feb. 15, 1835.
Trip, John & Fenny Manuel, Feb. 23, 1822 (Lic.).
Aug. 21, 1822.
Tubbs, John & Rachel Richison, Mar. 15, 1823 (Bond).
Berry Hill, BM.
Tucker, Goodman & Martha Tracy, Apr. 6, 1830 (Bond).
Tannehill Tracy, BM.
Tucker, Goodman & Martha Tracy, Apr. 6, 1830 (Lic.).
Apr. 10, 1830.
Tucker, Eli & Martha Tucker, Sept. 20, 1831 (Lic.).
Sept. 21, 1831.
Tucker, Jesse & Elizabeth Edleman, Jan. 3, 1831 (Bond).
William Tucker, BM.
Tucker, Jesse & Elizabeth Edleman, Jan. 3, 1831 (Lic.).
Jan. 3, 1831.
Turner, Benjamin & Margaret Chaffin, Jan. 18, 1832
(Lic.). Jan. 18, 1832.
Turner, James & Lovenia E. Cowin, Nov. 29, 1832 (Bond).
Robt. E. Halford, BM.
Turner, James & Lovenia E. Cowin, Nov. 29, 1832 (Lic.).
Nov. 29, 1832.
Turner, James H. & Rebecca F. Voss, July 12, 1836 (Bond).
A.M. Perkins, BM.

Turner, James H. & Rebecca F. Voss, July 12, 1838
(Lic.). July 12, 1836.
Turner, Jesse L. & Julena Sessums, May 29, 1824 (Lic.).
Turner, Thomas W. & Harriett T. Cayce, June 3, 1835
(Bond). Toliver P. Dalton, BM.

Ubbery, Henry & Pelina Brown, Feb. 14, 1838 (Bond).
Isaac Gibson, BM.
Ubbery, Henry & Pelina Brown, Feb. 14, 1838 (Lic.).
Feb. 15, 1838.

Vandiver, Edward & Nancy Wisdom, Oct. 23, 1825 (Bond).
B. Halford, BM.
Vincent, Merryman & Salina McCalister, July 19, 1838
(Bond). John Odom, BM.
Vincent, Merryman & Salina McCalister, July 19, 1838
(Lic.). July 19, 1838.
Voss, George & Polly Henderson, Jan. 8, 1832 (Bond).
William Porter, BM.
Voss, James & Rebeccah Harrelson, Mar. 10, 1820 (Bond).
William Harrelson, BM.
Voss, James & Rebeccah Harrelson, Mar. 10, 1820 (Lic.).
Mar. 12, 1820.
Voss, John & Jasindia Ashmore, Dec. 29, 1829 (Bond).
David Ratliff, BM.
Voss, John & Jasindia Ashmore, Dec. 29, 1829 (Lic.).
Jan. 4, 1830.
Voss, Leroy & Wada Simmons, Nov. 2, 1835 (Bond).
Duncan Buie, BM.
Voss, Leroy & Wada Simmons, Nov. 2, 1835 (Lic.).
Voss, Wiley & Elizabeth Farmer, July 26, 1825 (Bond).
William Voss, BM.
Voss, William & Sally Matthews, Aug. 4, 1821 (Bond).
John Matthews, BM.

Wade, William E. & Mary Johnston, Jan. 22, 1834 (Lic.).
Waggoner, Solomon & July Ann Day, Aug. 31, 1837 (Bond).
William Counce, BM.
Walden, Howell P. & Malinda McWhirter, Apr. 6, 1835
(Bond). Duncan Buie, BM.
Walden, Howell P. & Malinda McWhirter, Apr. 6, 1835
(Lic.). Apr. 6, 1835
Walker, Elijah & Elizabeth Gist, July 5, 1819 (Bond).
Joshua Gist, BM.
Walker, Elijah & Elizabeth Gist, Jan. 5, 1829 (Lic.).
Jan. 7, 1819.
(Wallace) Wallis, Bennet & Sally Vandiver, Aug. 2, 1819
(Bond). William Welch, BM.
Wallace, Joseph & Tahny Jane, July 22, 1826 (Bond).
Jesse Williams, BM.
Wallace, Thomas & Jane Christian, Aug. 15, 1823 (Bond).
James Teas, BM.
Wallis & Sally Vandiver, Aug. 2, 1819 (Bond).
William Welch, BM.

Walton, Ira & Dianah V. Sessums, Sept. 17, 1829 (Bond).
   Sept. 17, 1829.
Wasson, David H. & Ann Ray, Aug. 31, 1837 (Lic.).
   Aug. 30, 1837
Wasson, Eli J. & Angeline F. Voorhies, Sept. 11, 1838
   (Bond). William K. Sanford, BM.
Wasson, Eli J. & Angeline F. Voorhies, Sept. 11, 1838
   (Lic.). Sept. 11, 1838.
Wasson, James N. & Sarah K. Davidson, Jan. 21, 1834
   (Bond). William L. Wasson, BM.
Wasson, William L. & Jane Matthews, Jan. 8, 1835 (Bond).
   Samuel M. Wasson, BM.
Waters, John & Cinthy Mitchell, Sept. 19, 1831 (Bond).
   Robert Voss, BM
Waters, John & Cinthy Mitchell, Sept. 19, 1831 (Lic.).
   Sept. 19, 1831.
Watson, William S. & Rebecca Lewis, Dec. 1, 1834 (Bond).
   Samuel Harwell, BM.
Watson, William S. & Rebecca Lewis, Dec. 1, 1834 (Lic.).
   Dec. 1, 1834.
Weaver, Mark & Christeny Null, Mar. 5, 1818 (Bond).
   Phillip Null, BM.
Webb, Jackson & Nancy Beasley, June 25, 1832 (Bond).
   Wesley Shelton, BM.
Webb, Jesse & Hester Springer, Jan. 21, 1830 (Bond).
   Aaron Springer, BM.
Webb, Jesse & Hester Springer, Jan. 21, 1830 (Lic.).
   Jan. 25, 1830.
Weeks, Prewit & Nancy Burris, Apr. 7, 1838 (Lic.).
   Apr. 8, 1838.
Welch, James & Elizabeth Chronister, June 10, 1835
   (Bond). F.L.L. Carrell, BM.
Welch, Lyles & Susanna P. Mauldes, Sept. 23, 1838 (Lic.).
   Sept. 30, 1838.
Welch, Nicholas & Elizabeth Maxey, Mar. 1, 1819 (Lic.).
   Mar. 1, 1819.
Welch, Nicholas & Mary Clifton, Aug. 7, 1830 (Bond).
   Josiah S. Stockton, BM.
Welch, William & Sarah Bradshaw, Dec. 29, 1821 (Bond).
   Edward Mobley, BM.
Wester, John & Mary Smith, May 25, 1838 (Lic.).
   May 25, 1838.
Wharton, Caleb & Elizabeth Swaih, Dec. 1, 1821 (Lic.).
   Mar. 20, 1822.
Wharton, Caleb & (Name not shown), Dec. 1, 1836 (Bond).
   Henry S. Wilson, BM.
Wharton, John & Polly Hetamer, Oct. 20, 1823 (Bond).
   Meshack Inman, BM.
Wharton, John & Polly Hetamer, Oct. 30, 1823 (Lic.)
   Oct. 30, 1823.
White, Henry & Elizabeth McMasters, Jan. 3, 1838 (Bond).
   Wm. R. Gilbert, BM.
White, Henry & Elizabeth McMasters, Jan. 3, 1838 (Lic.).
   Jan. 4, 1838.

LAWRENCE COUNTY MARRIAGES

Whitefield, James M. & Eliza Belew, Feb. 23, 1833 (Bond).
    William R. Johnston, BM.
Whitefield, James M. & Eliza Belew, Feb. 23, 1833 (Lic.).
    Feb. 23, 1833.
Whitten, Joel & Nancy Gresham, Sept. 13, 1836 (Bond).
    Duncan Buie, BM.
Wiggs, John & Cathrine Hood, Feb. 15, 1836 (Bond).
    James Campbell, BM.
Wilburn, Ephraim & Mary Ann Newton, Sept. 23, 1837
    (Bond). Edmond Ezell, BM.
Wilburn, Ephraim & Mary Ann Newton, Sept. 23, 1837
    (Lic.). Sept. 23, 1837.
Willburn, James & Susannah Springer, Nov. 10, 1833
    (Bond). Peter P. Allsup, BM.
Williams, Bennett & Margaret Ray, Jan. 12, 1837 (Lic.).
    Jan. 12, 1837.
Williams, E.D. & Margaret A. Edmiston, May 5, 1836 ?
    (Bond). Stephen J. Matthews, BM.
Williams, E.D. & Margaret A. Edmiston, May 5, 1826
    (Lic.). May 5, 1826.
Williams, Jesse & Rebeccah Chaffin, Jan. 30, 1820
    (Bond). Nathaniel Morow, BM.
Williams, Spencer & Huldah Richards, Sept. 14, 1831
    (Lic.). Sept. 14, 1831.
Williams, Thomas & Jane Chaffin, Feb. 7, 1820 (Bond).
    John Chaffin, BM.
Williams, Zadock & Polly Herring, July 24, 1830 (Bond).
    Aaron Springer, Jr., BM.
Winchel, Uriah & Eliza Ann Richardson, Mar. 3, 1836
    (Bond). Edward Arnold, BM.
Wingow, Josiah & Jane Hunt, Dec. 19, 1835 (Lic.).
    Dec. 20, 1835.
Winters, Moses & Elizabeth Davis, Apr. 28, 1830 (Bond).
    Daniel Sailoers, BM.
Wisdom, James M. & Susan Paine, Apr. 14, 1828 (Bond).
    Edward Vandiver, BM.
Wisdom, James M. & Susan Paine, Apr. 16, 1828 (Lic.).
    Apr. 17, 1828.
Wisdom, Joseph & Martha Tucker, Aug. 28, 1832 (Lic.).
    Aug. 30, 1832.
Wisdom, William P. & Runey Nelson, Dec. 1, 1829 (Lic.).
    Dec. 2, 1829.
Wood, Thomas & Eliza Newton, Dec. 30, 1837 (Bond).
    Edmond Ezell, BM.
Wood, Thomas & Eliza Newton, Dec. 30, 1837 (Lic.).
    Dec. 30, 1837.
Woodruff, Ezell & Elizabeth Crow, July 29, 1823 (Bond).
    Elijah Mitchell, BM.
Woods, Lewis & Phoebe Jones, Mar. 13, 1824 (Bond).
    Phillip Jones, BM.
Woods, Lewis & Phoebe Jones, Mar. 13, 1824 (Lic.).
    Mar. 13, 1824.
Word, James & Sally Rosson, Mar. 9, 1837 (Lic.).
    Mar. 9, 1837.

Wortham, Alexander M. & Julia A. Wortham, Sept. 23, 1837
(Bond). Alsey Alford, BM.
Wright, D.W. & S.J. Hughes, Dec. 18, 1838 (Bond).
Joseph Miller, BM.
Wright, D.W. & S.J. Hughes, Dec. 18, 1838 (Lic.).
Dec. 18, 1838.
Wright, John E. & Martha Adkison, Sept. 10, 1836 (Bond).
John M. Adkison, BM.
Wright, John E. & Martha Adkison, Sept. 10, 1836 (Lic.).
Sept. 25, 1836.
Right, Lorenzo D. & Lucinda Hill, May 12, 1831 (Bond).
Tilman B. Parks, BM.

Yancey, Napolein B. & Lainer Garner, Aug. 11, 1837
(Bond). Thomas Yancey, BM.
Yarbrough, Humphrey & Milley Null, July 15, 1832 (Bond).
Annuel Adkisson, BM.
Yarbrough, Humphrey & Milley Null, July 15, 1832 (Lic.).
July 15, 1832.
Yates, John W. & Ann Moore, Feb. 3, 1825 (Lic.).
Feb. 6,. 1825.
Yearwood, William & Nancy Davis, July 11, 1838 (Bond).
James A. Turner, BM.
Yearwood, William & Nancy Davis, July 11, 1838 (Lic.).
July 11, 1838.
Young, John & Sally Willoughby, Feb. 29, 1832 (Bond).
Archibald Murphy, BM.
Young, John & Sally Willoughby, Feb. 29, 1832 (Lic.).
Mar. 3, 1832.

LAWRENCE COUNTY, TENNESSEE

Marriages, 1818-1854

Section 2: Marriage Record Book, 1838-1854

William G. Greenwood to Catherine Guest, Feb. 14, 1838
(Feb. 15, 1838).
Henry Irby to Pelina Brown, Feb. 14, 1838 (Feb. 15, 1838).
Aso O. Hartwick to Margaret Steal, Feb. 21, 1838.
Andrew J. James to Eliza Mason, Feb. 24, 1838 (Mar. 3, 1838).
Thomas Roberts to Nancy Simpson, Feb. 24, 1838 (Feb. 25, 1838).
Sparting Thornton to Mrs. Mary Johnston, Feb. 25, 1838.
John M. Brewer to Sarah Holloway, Feb. 27, 1838.
James McLaren to Cyntha Toys, Mar. 3, 1838 (Mar. 5, 1838).
Lewis Norman to Elizabeth M. Morris, Mar. 5, 1838
(Mar. 5, 1838).
George Baily to Elizabeth Rackly, Mar. 10, 1838 (Mar. 11,
1838).
Jesse Brumly to Sarah Hutchison, Mar. 21, 1838 (Mar. 12,
1838).
John W. Smith to Catherine Childress, Mar. 14, 1838
(Mar. 15, 1838).
Thos. J. Roberts to Martha Doyl, Mar. 23, 1838 (Mar. 26,
1838).
George Brewer to Martha Simms, Mar. 26, 1838.
Prewet Weeks to Nancy Burris, Apr. 7, 1838 (Apr. 8, 1838).
Turner Lanier to Louisa Templeton, Apr. 14, 1838.
Thomas A. Richardson to Lucy C. Burket, Apr. 23, 1838
(Apr. 24, 1838).
Woodford M. Lemay to Nancy Bashears, Apr. 28, 1838.
John Wester to Mary Smith, May 19, 1838 (May 25, 1838).
John F. Brown to Anna Wynick, May 24, 1838 (May 26, 1838).
Claburn Burks to Letiha Singleton, June 1, 1838 (June 1,
1838).
James C. Chapman to Martha Petty, June 7, 1838 (June 7,
1838).
William Swinney to Elizabeth Stewart, June 21, 1838
(July 2, 1838).
John Fondern to Mrs. Nancy McLean, June 26, 1838 (June
26, 1838).
Daniel McMasters to Barsheba Snodgrass, June 27, 1838.
John C. Richardson to Mary Ann May, June 30, 1838 (July
3, 1838).

LAWRENCE COUNTY MARRIAGES

John Bell to Eliza J. Duncan, June 3, 1838 (Aug. 3, 1838).
William Yearwood to Nancy Davis, July 11, 1838 (July 11, 1838).
Merriman Vinicent to Salina McCalister, July 19, 1838.
James Grissom to Elizabeth Blythe, Aug. 15, 1838.
Isaac Morris to Rebecca Davis, Aug. 27, 1838.
Eli Newburn to Nettie Shackleford, Aug. 29, 1838.
Braddock Lancaster to Cenith Vandiver, Aug. 29, 1838.
Eli J. Wasson to Angelina F. Vorhies, Sept. 11, 1838
(Sept. 11, 1838).
Josiah W. Rockley to Eliza Brown, Sept. 12, 1838 (Sept. 12, 1838).
Ephraim B. Greenhow to Angelina Foster, Sept. 12, 1838.
John A. Hail to Martha Sullivant, Mar. 21, 1838 (Mar. 22, 1838).
Jas. H. Carter to E. J. Richardson, Dec. 6, 1838 (Dec. 6, 1838).
Benjame Hensley to Lucinday Maner, June 10, 1839 (June 11, 1839).
Silas Merit to Lucinda Monday, June 26, 1839.
Charles Cook to Emarilla Bashers, June 19, 1839 (June 27, 1839).
Himbrick Sanders to Maria Davis, May 7, 1839.
John Cowers to Margret Burris, June 4, 1839 (June 4, 1839).
L. B. Kosure to Elizabeth Lucas, Mar. 24, 1839 (Mar. 24, 1839).
Lewallen Green to Nanny Bellew, Feb. 1, 1839 (Feb. 2, 1839).
A. W. Hagens to Mary A. Sharp, Feb. 6, 1839 (Feb. 6, 1839).
Stephen Jones to Marry M. Basham, Jan. 6, 1839 (Jan. 17, 1839).
Elisha P. Goble to Palina Mayhue, Jan. 18, 1839.
J. O. Strawn to Nancy Petty, Jan. 24, 1839 (Jan. 24, 1839).
Benjamine Crews to Elizabeth Stone, Feb. 16, 1839 (Feb. 16, 1839).
George Barnett to Lucinda Bowden, Feb. 11, 1839.
Burley W. Boswell to Mary Stribling, Feb. 16, 1839 (Feb. 27, 1839).
Wiley F. Bowden to Susanah Pollock, Nov. 7, 1839.
David Dalton to Mary Grisham, Dec. 20, 1839.
G. T. Matthews to Mary Stockard, May 12, 1839 (May 12, 1839).
S. Busby to M. R. McLean, Dec. 18, 1839 (Dec. 18, 1839).
William Hartwick to Nancy Weaver, Feb. 13, 1839 (Feb. 13, 1839).
W. R. Bell to Adaline Alexander, Apr. 25, 1839 (Apr. 25, 1839).
D. G. Grimes to Elizabeth Grisham, Feb. 4, 1839 (Feb. 7, 1839).
James M. Fogg to Juda Lewis, Apr. 6, 1839.
Jesse Higgs to Mahula White, Apr. 23, 1839 (Apr. 25, 1839).
Wm. Insor to Sally Brashears, Mar. 14, 1839.
Wm. Broadstreet to Eliza Markham, Mar. 16, 1839 (Mar. 17, 1839).
W. J. Shimpman to Elisabeth Altum, Mar. 6, 1839 (Mar. 13, 1839).

LAWRENCE COUNTY MARRIAGES

John Perry to Lanetty Turner, Mar. 8, 1839.
J.P. Haynes to J.L. McBride, Feb. 27, 1839 (Feb. 27, 1839).
Stanford Clayton to Nancy Crews, Feb. 27, 1839 (Feb. 26, 1839).
James M. Riddle to Mary King, Feb. 26, 1839 (Feb. 27, 1839).
John G. Clair to Winey Jones, Feb. 2, 1839 (Feb. 2, 1839).
Angis Campbell to M. Conly, Sept. 25, 1839 (Sept. 29, 1839).
Samuel Anderson to Dyara Cook, June 27, 1839.
H.D. Day to Marry Counts, June 27, 1839.
Levi Gist to Sally Heffington, July 2, 1839 (July 4, 1839).
John J. McCrackin to Louisa Lindsey, Mar. 20, 1839.
Samuel H. Martin to Maryan Black, July 23, 1839
   (July 25, 1839).
W.H. Futril to Unity Eskus, July 11, 1839 (July 10, 1839).
Philip Goats to Nancy Turnborough, Mar. 3, 1839 (Mar. 5,
   1839.
James Bell to Elisabeth Garner, Aug. 12, 1839 (Aug. 13, 1839).
Y.P. Roundtree to E.A. Johnston, Aug. 2, 1839 (Aug. 4, 1839).
John Counts to Lucretia Richardson, Sept. 7, 1839.
N.E. Bowdon to Marry Pollock, Aug. 13, 1839.
L.V. L.V. Skillern to Alitka Wilsford, Aug. 28, 1839
   (Aug. 29, 1839).
Wm. D. Bossham to Nancyann Hensly, Nov. 13, 1839.
Carrol Luker to Eliza Smith, Dec. 3, 1839.
R.L. Kelly to Evaline Hail, Aug. 20, 1839.
Wm. Grinway to C.K. Warrick, Nov. 19, 1839.
Wm. Boswell to Rachel Clayton, Oct. 21, 1839 (Oct. 22, 1839).
Charles Cook to Sarah Mason, Oct. 12, 1839 (Oct. 9, 1839).
John P. Fisher to Emily Brown, Oct. 5, 1839 (Sept. 22, 1839).
Richard Clayton to Elisabeth Gelespiee, Oct. 1, 1839
   (Oct. 1, 1839).
William Grigg to Marry Stephenson, Oct. 1, 1839.
Jonathan T. Pryor to Easter Boshears, Dec. 19, 1839.
   (Dec. 19, 1839).
Jas. J. Gibson to Mary Lucas, Oct. 17, 1839 (Oct. 17, 1839).
Wm. Montgomery to Susannah Cook, Sept. 21, 1839
   (Sept. 26, 1839).
Wm. Carroll to M.M. Strickland, Oct. 14, 1839 (Oct. 14, 1839).
Daniel Heffington to Ensson, Oct. 7, 1839.
Silas Merrit to Lourinda Monday, June 26, 1839
   (July 2, 1839).
Jesse Higgs to Caroline Grisham, Dec. 21, 1839.
D.P. Atkison to G.S. Lay, Dec. 12, 1839.
John Graham to Christian Weaver, Jan. 4, 1839.
Alford Mayhue to Ellen Campbell, Jan. 6, 1840.
John Gowers to Margaret Burris, June 4, 1839.
Carroll Kilbern to Milly Robertson, Dec. 17, 1839.
Burley W. Baswell to Marry Stribling, Feb. 26, 1839.
Wiley F. Bowden to Susanah Pollock, Nov. 7, 1839.
Elias P. Goble to Pauline Mayhue, Jan. 18, 1839.
Jas. McIntyre to H.C. Bumpass, Jan. 1, 1840.
Solomon Brewer to Eleanor Spencer, Nov. 12, 1839
   (Nov. 19, 1839).
William Baker to C. Rollantree, Jan. 31, 1839 (Jan. 31, 1839).
Stephen Jones to Mary M. Bassham, Jan. 16, 1839
   (Jan. 17, 1839).

J.D. Penington to Nancy S. Farrow, Dec. 23, 1839
(Dec. 26, 1839).
George Barnett to Loucinda Bowden, Feb. 11, 1839.
Benjamon Crews to Elizabeth Stone, Feb. 16, 1839.
W.C. Newton to Marry Green, June 6, 1840.
J.D. Christian to L. Blasengame, Jan. 4, 1840.
Gabe Bumpass to Mary Stribling, Dec. 31, 1839.
Jas. W. Welch to Nancy R. Mauldin, Jan. 25, 1840.
Jesse Barnet to Margaret Welch, Jan. 25, 1840 (Jan. 30, 1840).
J. Basham to T.M. Basham, Jan. 12, 1840.
Emanuel J. Kessel to Maryann Tidwell, Jan. 26, 1840
(Jan. 26, 1840).
Jesse Barnet to Margaret Welch, Jan. 25, 1840.
William Austin to Frances Pollock, Jan. 14, 1840.
L.L. Wood to Lucinda White, Jan. 25, 1840.
Samuel Burns to Eliz.Matthews, Oct. 22, 1839.
Jordon S. Campbell to Mary Ann Wise, Apr. 19, 1840
(Apr. --, 1840).
John R. Spears to Sarah Faught, May 18, 1840 (May 18, 1840).
Fed Green to Rutha Dial, June 18, 1840 (June 18, 1840).
R.C.E. Bateman to Rachel Philips, June 20, 1840
(June 21, 1840).
A.G. Osborn to Easter Hartwick, June 30, 1840 (June 30, 1840).
Warren Mason to Sarah Durbin, July 26, 1840 (July 26, 1840).
Nathan Keith to Ann Tooten, July 30, 1840 (July 30, 1840).
And. J. Jones to Charlotte Sullivant, Aug. 1, 1840
(Aug. 3, 1840).
L. Cossey to M. Cochran, Aug. 1, 1840.
G.W. Kimball to Sarah Guinn, Aug. 12, 1840 (Aug. 13, 1840).
W.E. Fisher to M. Adkison, Aug. 3, 1840.
W.G. Bradley to Caroline Wasson, Aug. 10, 1840 (Aug. 10,
1840).
D.J. Montgomery to Martha McHughs, Aug. 17, 1840
(Aug. 23, 1840).
Henry Bashears to Tabitha Stewart, Aug. 24, 1840
(Aug. 24, 1840).
Henry Reddell to Mary McCracken, Aug. 29, 1840
(Aug. 30, 1840).
Eli Bynam to Eleanor McDougal, Sept. 4, 1840 (Sept. 8, 1840).
Thomas Ethridge to Mary May, Sept. 7, 1840 (Sept. 10, 1840).
G.W. Grissom to Mahala Mayhu, Sept. 16, 1840 (Sept. 16, 1840).
Isaac Moton to Jane Guess, Sept. 16, 1840 (Sept. 17, 1840).
Stephen Cook to Louisa Cook, Sept. 13, 1840 (Sept. 23, 1840).
C.W. Cross to Sarah Ann Hall, Sept. 28, 1840 (Jan. 11).
William Cook to Susanah Cook, Oct. 2, 1840 (Oct. 2, 1840).
Alex S. Wortham to Elisibeth Smith, Nov. 2, 1840.
James E. Belew to Maryann Furguson, Nov. 5, 1840
(Nov. 5, 1840).
Smith Voss to Alfy Vaughter, Nov. 8, 1840 (Nov. 8, 1840).
R.C. Workman to Sarah C. Pickard, Nov. 27, 1840
(Nov. 29, 1840).
John Hays to Mary Williams, Nov. 16, 1840 (Nov. 19, 1840).
James K. Bennett to Lady Jane Devasure (Nov. 29, 1840
(Nov. 30, 1840).

LAWRENCE COUNTY MARRIAGES

John Sellers to Selina Ray, Dec. 1, 1840 (Dec. 9, 1840).
Everett A. Pearce to Mary Gilbreath, Dec. 30, 1840.
Sam Howard to Barbary Ratliff, Dec. 5, 1840 (Dec. 5, 1840).
William Bateman to Alsey Styles, Dec. 10, 1840 (Dec. 10, 1840).
Micajah McGee to Margaret Wisdom, Dec. 12, 1840 (Dec. 13, 1840).
William V. Glass to Elisabeth White, Dec. 12, 1840 (Dec. 14, 1840).
James Brumly to Elisabeth York, Dec. 12, 1840.
James Powel to Sarah L. Pullen, Dec. 14, 1840.
David Saterfield to Rebecca A. Grissham, Dec. 15, 1840 (Dec. 16, 1840).
Charles J. Dugger to Ethelinda L. Bumpass, Dec. 17, 1840 (Dec. 17, 1840).
Geo. D. Hillhouse to Eliza L. Alsup, Dec. 21, 1840 (Dec. 22, 1840).
G.M. Dickey to Phebe Powel, Dec. 21, 1840.
John Greenhaus to Milly Alford, Dec. 28, 1840 (Dec. 30, 1840).
Jesse Tucker to Milly Moore, Dec. 30, 1840.
James G. Sanford to Emeline A. Wasson, Dec. 31, 1840 (Dec. 31, 1840).
M.H. Moody to Mary Cook, Dec. 31, 1840.
M.F. McKinney to Lucinda Brashers, Mar. 23, 1841 (Apr. 5, 1841).
Thomas Wagoner to Charlott Miller, Jan. 5, 1841 (Jan. 5, 1841).
James C. Montgomery to Mary Hefly, Jan. 14, 1841.
Isaac McLusky to Martha A. Holland, Jan. 18, 1841 (Jan. 21, 1841).
Jno. W. Floyd to Mary Pollock, Jan. 19, 1841 (Jan. 19, 1841).
Elisha Bradly to Sarah Crews, Jan. 25, 1841 (Jan. 25, 1841).
Hugh McKnight to Melvina Williams, Feb. 4, 1841 (Feb. 4, 1841).
Jas. N. Curry to Elisa Thompson, Feb. 4, 1841.
Mark Richardson to Emeline May, Feb. 9, 1841 (Feb. 9, 1841).
Abner C. Williams to Elizabeth Pennington, Feb. 11, 1841 (Feb. 11, 1841).
William Foust to Mary Rosson, Feb. 25, 1841 (Feb. 28, 1841).
Esquire E. Choat to Nancy Atwell, Feb. 23, 1841 (Feb. 25, 1841).
Joseph Cook to Mary Ann Moody, Feb. 20, 1841.
Jno. J. Durly to Lutitia A. Lovel, Feb. 28, 1841 (Feb. 28, 1841).
Thos. Bryant to Mary Pullen, Mar. 9, 1841 (Mar. 10, 1841).
Sam Bradly to Moniah McEwin, Mar. 12, 1841 (Mar. 16, 1841).
N.H. Blasingam to Mary M. Matthews, Mar. 13, 1841 (Mar. 13, 1841).
Jno. P. Poteet to Frances F. Basham, Mar. 16, 1841 (Apr. 5, 1841).
A.T. Dobbin to Zilpha McMasters, Mar. 27, 1841 (Mar. 28, 1841).

Alley T. Vick to S.L. Norman, Apr. 6, 1841 (Apr. 6, 1841).
Addison Pope to Lena Blasingame, Apr. 12, 1841
(Apr. 12, 1841).
Wm. K. Sanford to W.N. Wasson, Apr. 14, 1841 (Apr. 15, 1841).
Ephraim White to D.C. Johnston, Apr. 22, 1841
(Apr. 22, 1841).
Jno. R. Spears to Sarah Faught, May 18, 1841.
Jarel Steen to Susannah Bilew, May 18, 1843 (May 18, 1843).
William Clemmons to Emeline Richardson, May 28, 1843
(May 28, 1843).
John Hagan to Martha Snodgrass, May 29, 1843 (June 18, 1843).
1843).
Peter   , June 5, 1841 (June 6, 1841).
Jonathan Markhan to Susanah Dueast, June 5, 1841
(June 5, 1841).
Winston McAnally to Caroline M. Smith, June 7, 1841
(June 10, 1841).
G.W. Sanders to Catharine Kilbarn, June 11, 1841 (June 13,
1841).
Josiah W. Kidd to Martha J. Chaffin, June 17, 1841
(June 17, 1841).
John Hamilton to Nancy B. Keenan, June 18, 1841
(June 18, 1841).
Thomas N. Williams to Julia F. Todd, June 24, 1841
(June 24, 1841).
Alex C. Pickard to Susan M. Blasingame, June 29, 1841
(June 30, 1841).
Samuel Garrett to E.M. Cosby, July 1, 1841 (July 6, 1841).
Richard Clayton to Mary A. Crews, Aug. 3, 1841 (Aug. 3, 1841).
Fenner J. Williams to Mary Hamlet, Aug. 3, 1838
(Aug. 3, 1838).
Alexr. Bowling to Isabella Simpson, Aug. 5, 1841
(Aug. 5, 1841).
Daniel Pain to Nancy C. Hunt, Aug. 8, 1841 (Aug. 8, 1841).
Jesse Depriest to Sarah Wasson, Aug. 11, 1841 (Aug. 11, 1841).
Mathew Hartwick to Malinda Cochran, Aug. 13, 1841
(Aug. 13, 1841).
William Rackley to Nancy M. Riddle, Aug. 14, 1841
(Aug. 17, 1841).
L. Mine Bentley to Araminta T. Arington, Aug. 25, 1841
(Sept. 23, 1841).
James G. Parter to Elizabeth Johnston, Aug. 25, 1841
(Sept. 2, 1841).
Matthew J. Swinney to Sarah Molton, Aug. 21, 1841
(Aug. 21, 1841).
Joel M. Alsup to Hannah McMasters, Aug. 28, 1841
(Aug. 28, 1841).
John Bentley to Jemime V. Hurst, Aug. 30, 1841 (Aug. 30,
1841).
John Grissom to Martha Redin, Aug. 30, 1841 (Sept. 3, 1841).
Nathan P. Hardin to Nicy Roberts, Sept. 1, 1841
(Sept. 1, 1841).
Aaron Comer to Ethamalinda Broshears, Sept. 1, 1841
(Sept 1, 1841).

LAWRENCE COUNTY MARRIAGES

Isaac Tidwell to Catherine Eaton, Sept. 6, 1841
(Sept. 6, 1841).
George P. Litteral to Catharine Holloway, Sept. 13, 1841
(Sept. 13, 1841).
F.P. Wasson to Sophia J. Campbell, Oct. 7, 1841
(Oct. 21, 1841).
Samuel S. Scott to Nancy Lay, Oct. 9, 1841 (Oct. 9, 1841).
John L. Dalton to Nancy Reddell, Oct. 17, 1841
(Oct. 7, 1841).
Elihu Voss to Isabella Craig, Oct. 13, 1841 (Oct. 14, 1841).
Harvey Daniel to Mary A. Clark, Oct. 26, 1841 (Oct. 26,
1841).
Jackson H. Hackney to E.A. Laffoon, Nov. 1, 1841.
Henry Prewitt to Eliza Adkins, Nov. 11, 1841 (Nov. 11, 1841).
James Tuttle to Malinda J. Dame, Nov. 11, 1841 (Nov. 11,
1841).
L.D. Snodgrass to Mary A. Rhea, Nov. 16, 1841 (Nov. 16,
1841).
Cader Baucum to Cynthia Ann Busby, Nov. 18, 1841
(Nov. 18, 1841).
William Dickson to Emelin Bivins, Nov. 18, 1841
(Nov. 18, 1841).
Geo. Shay to Priscilla Green, Nov. 21, 1841 (Nov. 22, 1841).
E.J. Bennet to Mary B. Rainey, Nov. 25, 1841 (Nov. 25, 1841).
William Simonton to Elizabeth Jane Allen, Nov. 24, 1841
(Nov. 24, 1841).
John Voss to Catharine Hunt, Nov. 27, 1841 (Nov. 30, 1841).
William N. Hamilton to Malissa Jane Yancy, Nov. 30, 1841
(Nov. 30, 1841).
William S. Duncan to Eleanor Williams, Dec. 2, 1841
(Dec. 21, 1841).
James Miles to Manerva Williams, Dec. 4, 1841 (Dec. 6, 1841).
Allen Long to Rebecca Ann Vorhies, Dec. 7, 1841
(Dec. 12, 1841).
Isaac W. Pennington to Eliza Dame, Dec. 7, 1841 (Dec. 7,
1841).
Stephen Moore to Nancy Tucker, Dec. 11, 1841.
John C. Goff to Margret K. Wood, Dec. 16, 1841 (Dec. 16,
1841).
Joel Kilborn to Emeline Davis, Dec. 21, 1841 (Jan. 3, 1842).
William B. Ball to Dicy E. Grissom, Dec. 22, 1841
(Dec. 22, 1841).
James Gist to Susannah Durbin, Dec. 28, 1841 (Dec. 30, 1841).
Joseph P. Layton to Reda Pollock, Dec. 29, 1841 (Jan. 5,
1842).
John Davidson to Lavine J. Layton, Dec. 29, 1841
(Feb. 14, 1842).
L. McNeill to Ann Gilmore, Dec. 30, 1841 (Dec. 30, 1841).
John McAnally to Amanda Wilsford, Dec. 31, 1841
(Jan. 4, 1842).
Samuel J. Riddell to Margaret J. Sullivant, Jan. 3, 1842
(Jan. 6, 1842).
William Ingram to Sarah Ann Green, Jan. 12, 1832
(Jan. 13, 1842).

41

LAWRENCE COUNTY MARRIAGES

Samuel Lay to Elizabeth Davis, Jan. 18, 1842 (Jan. 20, 1842).

William N. Wisdom to Ann J. Richardson, Jan. 18, 1842 (Jan. 18, 1842).

Obediah Lucre to Malinda Kelly, Jan. 19, 1842 (Jan. 19, 1842).

John C. May to Elizabeth Kelly, Jan. 19, 1842 (Jan. 20, 1842).

Hugh Nelson to Nancy Hunt, Jan. 24, 1842 (Jan. 24, 1842).

William A. Jones to Mary Grimes, Jan. 26, 1842 (Jan. 27, 1842).

Joel Dial to Sarah Lancaster, Jan. 29, 1842 (Jan. 30, 1842).

Moses McCann to Mary Green, Jan. 29, 1842 (Apr. 27, 1842).

Stephen A. Carrell to Mary F. Stribling, Feb. 2, 1842 (Feb. 4, 1842).

Nicholas Welch to Nancy Dame, Feb. 4, 1842 (Feb. 4, 1842).

O.T.D. Carter to A.M. Heffington, Feb. 11, 1842 (Feb. 13, 1842).

Willis J. Green to Elizabeth Canaway, Feb. 14, 1842 (Feb. 14, 1842).

Thomas Mitchell to Mary Barns, Feb. 16, 1842 (Feb. 20, 1842).

Sameul E. Mason to Sara Jane Clayton, Feb. 17, 1842.

William R. Walker to Mary E. Hefly, Feb. 23, 1842 (Feb. 20, 1842).

Fieldin Litteral to Lucy Woods, March 5, 1842.

John C. Sullivant to Mary Eleanor Riddell, Mar. 8, 1842 (Mar. 10, 1842).

Hilliard J. Thompson to Matilda Turner, Mar. 8, 1842 (Mar. 8, 1842).

George W. Pearce to Araminta Mitchell, Mar. 22, 1842 (Mar. 22, 1842).

Jacob Sanders to Sarah Carter, Mar. 28, 1842 (Mar. 31, 1842).

Daniel Davis to Lucinda Davis, Apr. 2, 1842 (Apr. 14, 1842).

Jesse Blyth to Parthena A. Pool, Apr. 6, 1842.

John S. Gilmore to Elizabeth Sims, Apr. 21, 1842 (Apr. 22, 1842).

James Jones to Elizabeth Wester, May 2, 1842 (May 4, 1842).

Allen Green to Sandel L. Cook, May 8, 1842.

Malachi Willis to Jane Couch, May 16, 1842 (May 18, 1842).

Francis Walker to Martha J. Pippins, May 24, 1842.

Robt. Williams to Mary Ann McCalister, May 25, 1842 (May 26, 1842).

John Grissam to Nancy McBride, May 29, 1842 (May 30, 1842).

Charles K. McLearen to Elizabeth Welch, May.

Samuel E. Mason to Sarah Jane Clayton, Feb. 17, 1842 (Feb. 17, 1842).

James W. Barnett to Martha Gilbert, June 13, 1842 (June 13, 1842).

John A. Lusk to America Canady, June 14, 1842 (June 16, 1842).

Samuel H. Bassham to Lucretia Miller, June 22, 1842 (June 24, 1842).

LAWRENCE COUNTY MARRIAGES

John M. Bailey to Parnecy Kelley, June 30, 1842
(June 30, 1842).
William Taylor to Maryan Tayler, July 8, 1842 (July 10,
1842).
John P. Miller to E. Richardson, July 20, 1842 (July 21,
1842).
Wiley B. Bishop to Mis G. Taylor, July 30, 1842 (Aug. 2,
1842).
John Carter to Rebecca Pope, Aug. 1, 1842.
Jerry Higgins to Sarah Fortenberry, Aug. 5, 1842
(Aug. 7, 1842).
George H. Nixon to Sarah E. Busby, Aug. 17, 1842
(Aug. 18, 1842).
Thos. J. Wheeler to Mary E. Lucas, Aug. 23, 1842
(Aug. 23, 1842).
William C. Floid to Frances Carter, Aug. 27, 1842
(Aug. 28, 1842).
Matthews Roach to Fanny Chapman, Aug. 31, 1842 (Aug. 31,
1842).
Solomon Wood to Martha Brown, Sept. 7, 1842.
Simeon Camfield to Elisabeth Williams, Sept. 9, 1842
(Sept. 9, 1842).
William F. Layton to Melvina Briley, Sept. 13, 1842.
Perry Myers to E.J. Hammonds, Sept. 15, 1842 (Sept. 28,
1842).
Hyram Appleton to S.D. Bassham, Sept. 17, 1842 (Sept. 22,
1842).
James M. Rose to Jane Ray, Sept. 20, 1842 (Sept. 22, 1842).
Mathew Hartsfield to Mary Holly, Sept. 21, 1842 (Sept. 22,
1842).
Lovick P. Parks to Caroline A. Dancy, Oct. 4, 1842
(Oct. 4, 1842).
Jacob Coker to Elizabeth Cawhorn, Oct. 4, 1842 (Oct. 4,
1842).
James H. Gilispie to Susan McKmillon, Oct. 8, 1842
(Oct. 12, 1842).
Kingston G. Banswell to Maryan Shackleford, Oct. 12, 1842
(Oct. 12, 1842).
Richard Polk to Joicy B. Linam, Oct. 13, 1842 (Oct. 13,
1842).
William C. May to Margret Jane Kelley, Oct. 18, 1842
(Oct. 20, 1842).
William Boaze to L.E. Richardson, Oct. 18, 1842 (Oct. 18,
1842).
Jesse Potts to Emaline Alexander, Oct. 19, 1842 (Oct. 20,
1842).
Raneney White to Catharine Rodgers, Oct. 23, 1842 (Oct. 24,
1842).
Philip Milton to Elizabeth Green, Oct. 23, 1842 (Oct. 25,
1842).
Lewis H. Smith to Catney Chapman, Oct. 28, 1842.
James M. Ramsy to Nancy A. McKnight, Nov. 1, 1842
(Nov. 1, 1842).
Eli Voss to Sarah F. Thompson, Nov. 10, 1842.

LAWRENCE COUNTY MARRIAGES

William W. Right to Mary Martin, Nov. 20, 1842 (Nov. 29, 1842).
Hugh Bride to M.A.P. Davis, Nov. 21, 1842 (Nov. 22, 1842).
John Rosebum to M.M. Thompkins, Nov. 23, 1842 (Nov. 23, 1842).
G.W. Calhoon to Rehico Sanders, Nov. 26, 1842.
John W. Pope to Rachal Poppe, Nov. 28, 1842 (Nov. 29, 1842).
Jeptha Newton to A.E. Hammonds, Nov. 29, 1842 (Nov. 30, 1842).
Jessee Brasures to Miss Schoals, Dec. 9, 1842 (Dec. 9, 1842).
A.F. Roberts to Cynthia E. Duncan, Dec. 26, 1842 (Dec. 26, 1842).
Wilson D. MckAnally to E.B. Murphy,
Berry Ham to Charity Blasenfim, Dec. 29, 1842 (Dec. 29, 1842).
Nathan C. Prior to Lucinda J. Boshears, Aug. 20, 1842 (Aug. 23, 1842).
Allen Richardson to Silvester Bolen, Jan. 10, 1843 (Jan. 12, 1843).
John W. Duncan to Mary A. McAnally, Jan. 26, 1843 (Jan. 26, 1843).
Joshua B. Ashmore to Levinch Hughs, Jan. 26, 1843 (Jan. 26, 1843).
Thomas J. Roberts to Juliann Bivens, Feb. 2, 1843 (Feb. 2, 1843).
John B. Dickson to E.J. Brown, Jan. 30, 1843 (Jan. 31, 1843).
Jas. C. Toys to Sarah F. Evans, Feb. 9, 1843.
Thomas C. Blasengim to T. Garden, Feb. 14, 1843 (Feb. 15, 1843).
G.C. Looker to Elizabeth Barnett, Feb. 18, 1843 (Feb. 19, 1843).
William P. Vaughan to Eliza Hill, Feb. 21, 1843 (Feb. 21, 1843).
Abraham Whitworth to Rhoda Gideon, Feb. 21, 1843 (Feb. 23, 1843).
Wm. Marcum to Mary C. Hammonds, Mar. 4, 1843 (Mar. 5, 1843).
W.C. Gordon to Elizabeth Ball, Nov. 7, 1842 (Nov. 8, 1842).
William Cochran to Malissa Odom, Sept. 14, 1842 (Sept. 18, 1842).
James Kilburn to Elizabeth McGee, Mar. 23, 1843 (Mar. 23, 1843).
G.B. Mitchell to Sarah M. Williams, Mar. 30, 1843.
Allen H. Bryan to Margaret Lindsey, Apr. 17, 1843.
L.G. Anderson to M.E. Haynes, Apr. 19, 1843 (Apr. 19, 1843).
James W. Bumpass to Lois D. McAnnally, May 3, 1843 (May 4, 1843).
Payton Manuel to Dicy Prior, May 20, 1843 (May 21, 1843).
Richard J. Bradley to Nancy Ingram, May 20, 1843 (May 21, 1843).
Joseph C. Inmon to Elizabeth A. Spears, May 30, 1843 (May 30, 1843).

44

LAWRENCE COUNTY MARRIAGES

Reddick Foster to Cyntha Brumley, June 13, 1843 (June 18, 1843).
Benjamin Walker to Ann White, July 12, 1843 (July 12, 1843).
John D. Davidson to Susan M. Wasson, July 17, 1843 (July 17, 1843).
Fountain R. Crabb to Elizath Brashers, July 19, 1843 (Jan. 1, 1844).
Nicholas J. Long to Cornelia J. Wortham, July 19, 1844 (July 20, 1844).
Elisha K. Pollock to Amanda Pickard, July 24, 1844 (July 26, 1844).
Jacob Copelin to A. Runnels, Jan. 28, 1843 (Feb. 7, 1843).
William J. Mobley to Eveline E. Hunt, Aug. 16, 1843 (Aug. 16, 1843).
Thomas T. Johnston to Rosannah Riddle, Aug. 21, 1843 (Aug. 23, 1843).
David Williams to Ursley Newton, Aug. 21, 1843 (Aug. 21, 1843).
John L. Baker to Luvina J. Layton, Aug. 25, 1843 (Aug. 31, 1843).
Fountain D. Hunt to Catharine B. McNeill, Aug. 30, 1843 (Aug. 30, 1843).
Saml H. Basham to Mary Jane Sheppard, Aug. 30, 1843 (Jan. 1, 1844).
James Philips to Rebecca Higdon, Sept. 1, 1843 (Sept. 1, 1843).
John Wood to Martha Jane Osburn, Sept. 9, 1843 (Sept. 10, 1843).
Elza Adkins to Permelia Walker, Sept. 14, 1843 (Sept. 14, 1843).
George Kelly to Elizabeth Jane Blair, Sept. 19, 1843 (Sept. 19, 1843).
Daniel M. Ball to Mary A.E. Cross, Sept. 27, 1843 (Sept. 28, 1843).
Saml Johnston to Martha Freeman, Oct. 3, 1843 (Oct. 3, 1843).
Jackson Cockerel to Sarah Tooten, Oct. 5, 1843 (Oct. 5, 1843).
John Brice to Susannah G. Branch, Sept. 28, 1843.
Joseph M. Pennington to Martha Kirk, Oct. 11, 1843 (Oct. 12, 1843).
Berry C. Overstreet to Mary Campbell, Oct. 31, 1843 (Oct. 31, 1843).
John E. Ham to Sarah Ann Mitchell, Dec. 2, 1843 (Dec. 3, 1843).
H.R. Sharp to Sarah J. Harrison, Nov. 9, 1843 (Nov. 9, 1843).
Solon E. Eose to Marcella Buchanon, Nov. 11, 1843 (Nov. 14, 1843).
A.G. Shannon to Jane Edwards, Nov. 13, 1843 (Nov. 14, 1843).
Robert Farriss to Mary C. Kenneddy, Nov. 16, 1843 (Nov. 16, 1843).
James Pullen to Martha Ann Lindsey, Nov. 17, 1843.

45

James B. Kidd to Sarah Wilcoxin, Dec. 2, 1843 (Dec. 3, 1843).

George W. Tole to Elizabeth Armstrong, Dec. 2, 1843.

Wm. Waldroup to Mary Saylors, Dec. 14, 1843.

John Riddle to Anne Sullivant, Dec. 26, 1843.

Haywood Keith to Arena Myers, Dec. 22, 1843 (Dec. 24, 1843).

Abraham Helton to Mary A. Duncan, Dec. 26, 1843 (Dec. 26, 1843).

B.F. Osborn to Ruhahar Delozier, Dec. 26, 1843 (Dec. 26, 1843).

Isaac Chennault to Eliz L. Vandiver, Dec. 29, 1843 (Dec. 30, 1843).

Elijah Dicus to Mahala Austin, Jan. 13, 1844 (Jan 13, 1844).

Joseph Bailey to Nancy N. Williams, Jan. 11, 1844 (Jan. 11, 1844).

John Beaths to Mary Poplin, Jan 13, 1844 (Jan. 14, 1844).

Richard Spears to Elizabeth Kilburn, Feb. 5, 1844.

W.T. Buchanan to Isabella Jane Davis, Feb. 6, 1844 (Feb. 6, 1844).

John H. Lucus to Martha E. Morris, Feb. 6, 1844.

Samuel Marcum to Nancy M. Vawter, Feb. 13, 1844 (Feb. 13, 1844).

John Davis to Sarah Hughs, Jan. 17, 1844 (Jan. 17, 1844).

John W. Barner to Amanda Evans, Feb. 14, 1844 (Feb. 15, 1844).

Jackson J. Morris to Maria Lee, Feb. 16, 1844 (Feb. 18, 1844).

Andrew J. Lindsey to Tabitha Ann Sullivant, Mar. 5, 1844.

John H. Riggs to Rachael Arritta Perrymore, Feb. 27, 1844 (Feb. 28, 1844).

Robt. N. Samford to Martha J. Turner, Mar. 10, 1844 (Mar. 10, 1844).

Jesse Earwood to Lucinda Smith, Apr. 24, 1844 (Apr. 26, 1844).

Joseph Tice to Lucinda Riddle, Apr. 25, 1844 (Apr. 25, 1844).

William D. Kelton to Elizabeth M. Wall, May 1, 1844 (May 2, 1844).

D.L. Duncan to Eliz. Miatt, May 4, 1844 (May 5, 1844).

William F. Basham to Dinah B. Hail, May 7, 1844 (May 9, 1844).

Higah Hughes to Nancy Earwood, May 20, 1844 (May 21, 1844).

David W. Strayhorn to Sarah A.L. Lynam, May 21, 1844 (May 21, 1844).

Joseph Spears to Mary Ann L. Warton, May 28, 1844 (May 28, 1844).

Charles L. McLean to Mary E. Abernathy, Apr. 15, 1844 (Apr. 15, 1844).

Jasper Smith to Cassey Ann K. Myers, May 31, 1844 (May 31, 1844).

N.B. Gibbons to Eliz. A. Basham, June 3, 1844 (June 3, 1844).

James M. Short to Elizabeth White, Jan. 14, 1844.

LAWRENCE COUNTY MARRIAGES

John C. Innman to Mary A. Lyles, Mar. 9, 1844 (Mar. 10, 1844).
William H. Coffman to Rebecca Petty, Apr. 29, 1844 (Apr. 29, 1844).
Pleasant Holloway to Sarah Williams, Apr. 15, 1844 (Apr. 15, 1844).
John W. Hail to Mary Kelly, June 10, 1844.
George W. Foster to P.A. Mobley, June 26, 1844 (June 27, 1844).
William Howard to Elizabeth Lucus, July 4, 1844 (July 4, 1844).
James Craig to Margaret M. Vorhies, July 16, 1844.
Stephen Green to Elizabeth Dial, May 14, 1844 (May 14, 1844).
William C. Crofford to Rosalinds Tinnon, July 20, 1844 (July 20, 1844).
Wm. C. Moores to Elizabeth Holloway, Aug. 5, 1844 (Aug. 7, 1844).
Franklin C. Allen to Lucy Ann Buchanan, Aug. 19, 1844 (Aug. 22, 1844).
Benjamin Wood to Eliza Hamersley, Aug. 20, 1844 (Aug. 22, 1844).
George W. Cookburne to Harriet Jane Goff, Sept. 3, 1844 (Sept. 3, 1844).
Eli H. Alford to Eliz. J. Hanner, Sept. 4, 1844 (Sept. 5, 1844).
Laban Grissom to Emeline Mayhew, Aug. 12, 1844 (Aug. 16, 1844).
John Sailors to Malinda Lancaster, Sept. 9, 1844 (Sept. 9, 1844).
Hezekiah Brown to Milberry Jane Lewis, Sept. 11, 1844 (Sept. 12, 1844).
John H. Riddle to Angeline Horn, Sept. 16, 1844 (Sept. 17, 1844).
James F. Henderson to Isabella Jane Gaither, Sept. 16, 1844 (Sept. 16, 1844).
Roford F. Pearce to Elender Jane White, Sept. 18, 1844 (Sept. 24, 1844).
Robert E. Barnes to Mary F.E. Kirk, Sept. 18, 1844 (Sept. 18, 1844).
James Turnbow to Hannah Freeman, Sept. 23, 1844 (Sept. 23, 1844).
Jonas Crews to Mary V. Hensley, Sept. 23, 1844 (Sept. 24, 1844).
Noble Osburn to Emeline Short, Sept. 19, 1844 (Sept. 19, 1844).
John Campbell to Catherine Trorbaugh, Sept. 22, 1844 (Sept. 22, 1844).
William C. Riddle to Cynthia A. Riddle, Sept. 28, 1844 (Oct. 10, 1844).
Alexander Miller to Mary McMasters, Oct. 2, 1844 (Oct. 3, 1844).
Harlow A. Tripp to Elizabeth Alford, Oct. 9, 1844 (Oct. 9, 1844).

47

Jacob W. Pennington to Mahala Dame, Oct. 9, 1844 (Oct. 9, 1844).
James Robertson to Lucinda Leigh, Oct. 15, 1844.
Asa D. Mewborn to Lucinda Mewborn, Oct. 27, 1844.
Robert J. Kelly to Emily J. Abernathy, Oct. 20, 1844 (Oct. 20, 1844).
Greenberry Shelton to Alpha Cotrell, Oct. 31, 1844 (Oct. 31, 1844).
Jesse Potts to Margaret Hill, Nov. 2, 1844 (Nov. 3, 1844).
Levi Voss to Sarah Pennington, Nov. 4, 1844 (Nov. 4, 1844).
Joseph Hughes to Mary Underwood, Nov. 9, 1844 (Nov. 10, 1844).
Thomas J. McCrory to Wady Tripp, Nov. 9, 1844 (Nov. 10, 1844).
Thomas Wilsford to Sarah Blair, Nov. 23, 1844 (Nov. 24, 1844).
Lewis Gulley to Elizabeth Bromley, Dec. 4, 1844 (Dec. 9, 1844).
Green B. Curry to Margaret Thompson, Dec. 11, 1844 (Dec. 11, 1844).
William H. Hensley to Catharine Powel, Dec. 18, 1844.
George Murphy to Sally Jones, Dec. 19, 1844 (Dec. 19, 1844).
George A. Brown to Nancy L. Kilburn, Dec. 28, 1844 (Dec. 31, 1844).
James A. Riddle to Mariah Ethridge, Jan. 1, 1845 (Jan. 9, 1845).
Wm. Richardson to Elizabeth Ann Chaffin, Jan. 8, 1845 (Jan. 8, 1845).
George O. Hunt to Amanthus M. Riddle, Jan. 9, 1845 (Jan. 9, 1845).
J.H.L. Anderson to Sarah Bingham, Jan. 9, 1845 (Jan. 9, 1845).
Jesse F. Sanders to Mary Ann Perrymore, Jan. 25, 1845 (Jan. 27, 1845).
James D. McBride to Julia Monday, Jan. 28, 1845 (Jan. 28, 1845).
Nace Green to Mahala Richards, Jan. 29, 1845 (Feb. 1, 1845).
Silas Tidwell to Rachel E. McMasters, Feb. 3, 1845 (Feb. 4, 1845).
Samuel Howard to Malinda Ratliff, Feb. 13, 1845 (Feb. 13, 1845).
John H. Vandiver to Martha Roberts, Feb. 10, 1845.
Wm. Kelly to Eliza Ann Tracy, Feb. 17, 1845 (Feb. 18, 1845).
Nicholas Gower to Frances D. Bumpass, Feb. 18, 1845 (Feb. 18, 1845).
Dice Riggin to Arbina Garner, Feb. 22, 1845 (Feb. 27, 1845).
James R. Kelso to Elizabeth Rea, Feb. 22, 1845 (Mar. 1, 1845).
Calvin Sanders to Fanny Kilburn, Mar. 14, 1845 (Mar. 15, 1845).

LAWRENCE COUNTY MARRIAGES

Jackson Hinson to Adaline Cross, Mar. 18, 1845 (Mar. 20, 1845).
William Joyce to Rebecca Watson, Mar. 22, 1845 (Mar. 22, 1845).
William Burlow to Eliza Osburn, Apr. 1, 1845 (Apr. 1, 1845).
Leroy McGee to Martha Clayton, Apr. 3, 1845 (Apr. 10, 1845).
Samuel Campbell to Margaret Kelly, Apr. 4, 1845 (Apr. 4, 1845).
Enoch G. Johns to Amanda F. Wiggs, Apr. 5, 1845 (Apr. 6, 1845).
Joseph Bishop to Elizabeth Lewis, Apr. 5, 1845 (Apr. 6, 1845).
Judge C. Rickman to Leletha Ann Holland, Apr. 13, 1845 (Apr. 17, 1845).
James B. Buckitt to Mary Richardson, Apr. 17, 1845 (Apr. 17, 1845).
Washington Snow to Frances Kilburn, Apr. 24, 1845.
Charles H. Wolf to Rosilla H. Steward, Apr. 29, 1845 (Apr. 30, 1845).
Samuel Escue to Almira Jane Hendrix, May 28, 1845 (May 29, 1845).
Simon Hendrix to Mary Howard, May 28, 1845 (May 29, 1845).
John W. Pennington to Louisa V. Bailey, June 14, 1845 (June 17, 1845).
John Jackson to Susan G. Skillern, July 26, 1845.
Richard Harvey to Elizabeth Ham, July 1, 1845 (July 3, 1845).
John A. Kidd to Manerva Ann Pullen, July 3, 1845 (July 3, 1845).
Abraham Whitworth to Hannah Kelly, July 11, 1845 (July 11, 1845).
James M. Grisom to Eliza C. Chapman, July 15, 1845 (July 16, 1845).
John Sullivant to Sarah M. Riddell, July 22, 1845 (July 24, 1845).
William Carrell to Elendor Jones, July 22, 1845 (July 24, 1845).
William E. Grisham to Nancy F. Gordon, Aug. 2, 1845 (Aug. 6, 1845).
Philip G. Austin to Mary Johnston, Aug. 25, 1845 (Aug. 26, 1845).
William Osburn to Elizabeth Glover, Sept. 6, 1845 (Sept. 7, 1845).
Thomas J. Gabel to Mary Stewart, Sept. 8, 1845 (Sept. 9, 1845).
Joseph E. Bailey to Dovey C. Lucus, Sept. 9, 1845 (Sept. 9, 1845).
Reuben Gooden to Sally McGwire, Sept. 24, 1845 (Sept. 25, 1845).
John B. Martin to Winneford Pearce, Sept. 26, 1845 (Sept. 30, 1845).
Daniel W. May to Martha C. Martin, Oct. 1, 1845 (Oct. 1, 1845).

LAWRENCE COUNTY MARRIAGES

Jasper Willbourn to Sarah Jane Broshears, Oct. 6, 1845
(Oct. 6, 1845).
Edward Lovell to Ritta Fullington, Oct. 9, 1845 (Oct. 9,
1845).
David Lindsey to Margaret A. Grissom, Oct. 16, 1845
(Oct. 16, 1845).
Albert W. Riggs to Jane Adaline Perrymore, Oct. 16, 1845
(Oct. 16, 1845).
Thomas D. Lyles to Elizabeth Holt, Oct. 18, 1845 (Oct. 19,
1845).
Wm. C. Blair to Sarah E. McLaren, Oct. 22, 1845 (Oct. 22,
1845).
James Harlow to Sarah Prier, Oct. 25, 1845 (Oct. 25, 1845).
Abrin Smith to Mariah McAnnally, Oct. 28, 1845 (Oct. 28,
1845).
William F. Harrison to Nancy C. Montgomery, Oct. 28, 1845
(Oct. 28, 1845).
Samuel Brasier to Mary Kilburn, Nov. 3, 1845 (Nov. 4, 1845).
Hubbard Hodge to Malissa Maimon, Nov. 4, 1845 (Nov. 4,
1845).
Isaac N. Craig to Rebecca R. Williams, Nov. 5, 1845
(Nov. 5, 1845).
John W. Pollock to Rebecca M. Morris, Nov. 8, 1845 (Nov. 12,
1845).
John W. Morris to Eveline J. Pollock, Nov. 8, 1845 (Nov. 12,
1845).
Robert Tayes to Catharine Walker, Nov. 13, 1845 (Nov. 13,
1845).
Alfred D. Wiley to Jane Blythe, Nov. 16, 1845 (Nov. 16,
1845).
James F. Crews to Jane Shipman, Nov. 19, 1845 (Nov. 19,
1845).
William M. Ham to Eliza Blasingame, Nov. 21, 1845 (Nov. 21,
1845).
Moses H. Willis to Eliza McDougal, Nov. 26, 1845 (Nov. 27,
1845).
Charles H. Myers to Catharine Stewart, Dec. 1, 1845
(Dec. 1, 1845).
James M. Bassham to Mary Ann Johnson, Dec. 4, 1845
(Dec. 11, 1845).
Francis M. McAnnally to Margaret Dame, Dec. 7, 1845
(Dec. 7, 1845).
Charles J. Burney to E.M.M. Richards, Dec. 12, 1845
(Dec. 12, 1845).
Jackson Grimes to Sara Ann Smith, Dec. 12, 1845 (Dec. 12,
1845).
Granville T. Wilsford to Evaline K. Stribling, Dec. 13,
1845 (Dec. 16, 1845).
Booker Bailey to Jane Nelson, Dec. 16, 1845 (Dec. 17,
1845).
William C. Best to Mary E. Gordon, Dec. 18, 1845 (Dec. 21,
1845).
Joseph W. Couch to Kiziah E. Haynes, Dec. 23, 1845
(Dec. 23, 1845).

LAWRENCE COUNTY MARRIAGES

Wm. R. Mitchell to Jane Barnett, Dec. 25, 1845
(Dec. 25, 1845).
Jacob M. Pennington to Mariah Morrow, Jan. 1, 1845
(Jan. 1, 1845).
Philip M. Pennington to Sara F. Morrow, Jan. 5, 1845
(Jan. 11, 1845).
Melchesedick McLean to Mary Jane McLaren, Jan. 7, 1845
(Jan. 8, 1845.
John Robertson to Mary Marcum, Jan. 8, 1845 (Jan. 8, 1845).
Barnett Spears to Angeline Ratliff, Jan. 13, 1845.
Raiford Burkes to Frances Gunter, Jan 21, 1845 (Jan. 22,
1845).
William M. Dickie to Nancy Hamlet, Jan. 22, 1845
(Jan. 22, 1845).
Nicholas Spears to Elizabeth Wharton, Jan. 22, 1845
(Jan. 22, 1845).
William Ratliff to Mary Spears, Jan. 28, 1845 (Jan. 29,
1845).
George A. Davis to Louise Wharton, Feb. 3, 1845 (Feb. 3,
1845).
Wm. C. Barnes to Barbary J. Pickard, Feb. 5, 1845
(Feb. 5, 1845).
Riley M. Melton to Priscilla H. Green, Feb. 12, 1845
(Feb. 12, 1845).
Fenner J. Williams to Sarah Whitehead, Feb. 12, 1845
(Feb. 12, 1845).
Wm. W. Thornton to Susan Tucker, Mar. 4, 1845 (Mar. 4,
1845).
James York to Mary E. Due-East, Mar. 6, 1845 (Mar. 8, 1845).
James Weaver to Sarah Jane Goad, Mar. 7, 1846 (Mar. 8,
1846).
Leonidas M. Bently to Martha A. Moore, Mar. 9, 1846
(Mar. 9, 1846).
William P. Horne to Mary M. Stribling, Mar. 10, 1846
(Mar. 10, 1846).
Ephraim Greenhaw to Rebecca Ethridge, Mar. 10, 1846
(Mar. 12, 1846).
Spencer A. Bevers to Mary Jane Fuller, Mar. 11, 1846
(Mar. 12, 1846).
William Morris to Nancy L. Keltner, Mar. 28, 1846
(Mar. 29, 1846).
Jonathan Crews to Frances Morrow, Apr. 7, 1846 (Apr. 7,
1846).
Henry McGree to Margret Ann Gallaher, Apr. 15, 1846
(Apr. 15, 1846).
Alexander W. McMillon to Elendor Pursell, Apr. 23, 1846
(Apr. 24, 1846).
Thomas W. Sharber to Malinda Lyons, Apr. 26, 1846
(Apr. 30, 1846).
David Petty to Nancy Bryan, Apr. 27, 1846 (Apr. 30, 1846).
Calvin L. Herbert to Nancy Deavenport, May 5, 1846
(May 5, 1846).
Isaac G. Barr to Elizabeth Martin, May 12, 1846 (May 12,
1846).

51

Franklin Snow to Elizabeth Kilburn, May 14, 1846
(May 14, 1846).
John Williams to Hannah Wood, May 26, 1846 (May 26, 1846).
Isaac A. Hale to Martha Johnston, May 27, 1846 (May 27,
1846).
Caloway McGee to Eliza Ann Gower, May 27, 1846 (May 27,
1846).
Henderson Burgess to Lucy A. Young, June 5, 1846
(June 5, 1846).
Tanneyhill Tracy to Nancy Bingham, June 9, 1846 (June 9,
1846).
Thomas Holden to Manerva Williams, June 10, 1846 (June 11,
1846).
Wm. A. Altum to Mary Eliz. Roach, June 17, 1845 (June 18,
1846).
Zachariah Crews to Eliza J. Ponds, June 25, 1846 (June 26,
1846).
Alfred Smith to Eliza J. Pullen, June 26, 1846.
Howard Hale to Mahulda Williams, June 27, 1846 (Oct. 1,
1846).
Wiley Hoke to Mary E. Deavenport, July 9, 1846 (July 9,
1846).
James M. Brewer to Elizabeth Parker, July 13, 1846 (July 15,
1846).
Samuel Osburn to Martha Green, July 14, 1846 (July 14, 1846).
Arthur R. Chronister to Candace Pennington, July 20, 1846
(July 21, 1846).
William R. Spears to Isabella Simpson, July 23, 1846
(July 27, 1846).
James H. Newton to Adelia Wilbourn, July 27, 1846 (July 29,
1846).
Alexander Harvell to Rebecca Ann Rosson, Aug. 1, 1846
(Aug. 3, 1846).
Hensley Carpenter to Louisa Tomlinson, Aug. 5, 1846
(Aug. 6, 1846).
John S. Gaither to Sarah E. Stribling, Aug. 10, 1846
(Aug. 13, 1846).
Zachariah Belew to Sarah Ann Newton, Aug. 14, 1846
(Aug. 16, 1846).
Richard Fields to Sarah Jane Johnston, Sept. 1, 1846
(Sept. 3, 1846).
Elias Jones to Sarah M. Hamilton, Sept. 2, 1846 (Sept. 3,
1846).
Alexander Whitley to Jane Higgs, Sept. 12, 1846 (Sept. 12,
1846).
John J. Brewer to Jalina Parker, Sept. 14, 1846 (Sept. 17,
1846).
Robert Hodge to Rachael E. Smith, Sept. 17, 1846 (Sept. 17,
1846).
William R. McGee to Catharine C. Gower, Sept. 17, 1846
(Sept. 17, 1846).
Amos Goodman to Louisa Hill, Oct. 10, 1846 (Oct. 11, 1846).
John McMackin to Elizabeth Cockeral, Oct. 16, 1846
(Oct. 16, 1846).

LAWRENCE COUNTY MARRIAGES

William Prier to Martha Martila Brashers, Oct. 20, 1846
(Oct. 20, 1846).
Joseph Barin to Sarah York, Oct. 23, 1846 (Oct. 24, 1846).
Holman Bird to Elizabeth Adkison, Oct. 24, 1846 (Oct. 25,
1846).
George W. Morris to Matilda Johns, Oct. 26, 1846 (Oct. 28,
1846).
Joseph R. Bradley to Emily Greenhaw, Oct. 29, 1846 (Oct. 29,
1846).
Benjamin J. Vick to Delila Riddle, Nov. 11, 1846 (Nov. 12,
1846).
Ezra Cates to Martha A. Pickard, Nov. 11, 1846 (Nov. 11,
1846).
John L. Emerson to Eleanor Jane Chambers, Nov. 12, 1846
(Nov. 12, 1846).
Nicholas Saylors to Nancy Lancaster, Nov. 19, 1846 (Nov. 19,
1846).
William A. Gower to Susannah McGee, Nov. 21, 1846 (Nov. 22,
1846).
A.B. Meredith to Chaney Clement, Nov. 28, 1846 (Nov. 28,
1846).
Levi H. Bateman to Jane Ray, Nov. 30, 1846.
L.M. Sanford to Mary E. Wooten, Dec. 9, 1846 (Dec. 9, 1846).
Winston Arnold to Sarah C. Hill, Dec. 10, 1846 (Dec. 10,
1846).
William Davis to Nancy Gwinn, Dec. 12, 1846 (Dec. 13, 1846).
Rufus Rochell to Mary C. Osborn, Dec. 12, 1846 (Dec. 15,
1846).
John R. Pearce to Mary A. Higgs, Dec. 14, 1846 (Dec. 16,
1846).
John Gist to Elizabeth Fisher, Jan. 2, 1847 (Jan. 3, 1847).
Joseph E. Rogers to Eveline Lindsey, Jan. 5, 1847 (Jan. 5,
1847).
Patrick Flippo to Rebecca Skillern, Jan. 5, 1847.
James H. Crabb to Dicey Brashers, Jan. 7, 1847 (Jan. 7,
1847).
Sidney Crews to Mary Ann Ponds, Jan. 11, 1847 (Jan. 12,
1847).
Philip F. Bashers to Archaday Beard, Jan. 14, 1847
(Jan. 14, 1847).
James Poteet to Nancy Williams, Jan. 14, 1847 (Jan. 17,
1847).
William Brown to Catharine Mires, Jan. 18, 1847 (Jan. 19,
1847).
Benjamin F. Mauldin to Mary Welch, Jan. 18, 1847 (Jan. 21,
1847).
Newton A. Carrell to Mariah Bailey, Jan. 25, 1847 (Jan. 28,
1847).
George Moore to Barbary Ballard, Jan. 27, 1847 (Jan. 27,
1847).
James M. Breckinridge to Elizabeth M. Colier, Jan. 28,
1847 (Jan. 28, 1847).
William J. Fuller to Mary B. Davidson, Jan. 28, 1847
(Jan. 28, 1847).

Robert Newton to Malissa Ann White, Feb. 9, 1847 (Feb. 17, 1847).

Anderson M. Fisher to Celia Ann Hartsfield, Feb. 16, 1847 (Feb. 18, 1847).

Richard Campbell to Adelia McMackin, Feb. 20, 1847 (Feb. 21, 1847).

Thomas H. Lawhon to Mary White, Feb. 22, 1847 (Feb. 22, 1847).

Isaac Cox to Manerva Garrett, Feb. 23, 1847 (Feb. 23, 1847).

Wm. H. Simmons to Mary A. Durbin, Feb. 24, 1847 (Feb. 25, 1847).

Lewis Seaton to Elizabeth Miles, Feb. 26, 1847 (Feb. 26, 1847).

John Bell to Agnes Jane Birch, Feb. 26, 1847 (Mar. 2, 1847).

William H. Williams to Susan C. Smith, Mar. 1, 1847 (Mar. 2, 1847).

Jesse M. Bruce to Louisa Jane Smith, Mar. 1, 1847 (Mar. 2, 1847).

Daniel A. Stewart to Caroline Spain, Mar. 2, 1847 (Mar. 3, 1847).

James M. Chapman to Lucinda Rackley, Mar. 18, 1847 (Mar. 18, 1847).

James Williams to Elizabeth Gray, Apr. 8, 1847 (Apr. 8, 1847).

Micajah Davis to Manerva Jane Holt, Apr. 8, 1847 (Apr. 11, 1847).

George W. Kimbrel to Mary Gwinn, Apr. 8, 1847 (Apr. 10, 1847).

Charles Campbell to Nancy Craig, Apr. 17, 1847 (Apr. 18, 1847).

David Cox to Marinda McCewen, Apr. 19, 1847 (Apr. 19, 1847).

Dickson Tucker to Martha Welch, Apr. 22, 1847 (May 2, 1847).

John N. Porter to Mrs. Mariah Smith, Apr. 28, 1847 (Apr. 28, 1847).

James T. Caldwell to Lucy M. Lynan, May 5, 1847 (May 5, 1847).

Felix G. Morris to Henrietta C. Pollock, May 21, 1847 (May 22, 1847).

Robert N. Warren to Mary Ann Kelly, June 8, 1847 (June 8, 1847).

Nicholas Terry to Martha Clifton, June 10, 1847 (June 10, 1847).

Alphonso Willis to Dicey Davis, June 12, 1847 (June 13, 1847).

Shadrack Hackley to Nancy Shaw, June 22, 1847.

Wm. C. Martin to Sarah Jane Clay, July 1, 1847.

Pleasant Massey to Mary Jane Foster, July 19, 1847 (July 19, 1847).

Benjamin W. Moore to Catharine A. Caldwell, July 20, 1847 (July 21, 1847).

Thomas W. Moss to Sarah Tyler, July 22, 1847.

Jesse B. Kirksey to Adaline Smith, July 25, 1847 (July 25, 1847).

LAWRENCE COUNTY MARRIAGES

Zerubbabel Crook to Mary J.E. McLaren, July 28, 1847
(July 29, 1847).
Dickson Spears to Milly A.P. Warton, Aug. 5, 1847 (Aug. 5,
1847).
Elihu M. Chaffin to Lenora P. Wisdom, Aug. 5, 1847 (Aug. 5,
1847).
Elijah Melton to Elizabeth Hunt, Aug. 6, 1847 (Aug. 7,
1847).
David Kilburn to Elizabeth Spears, Aug. 7, 1847.
James M. Johnston to Ann R. Bruce, Aug. 8, 1847 (Aug. 9,
1847).
Edward Murphy to Milly Ray, Aug. 11, 1847.
George Carr to Amanda E.A. Chambers, Aug. 12, 1847
(Aug. 12, 1847).
Daniel M. Stewart to Sarah F. Tays, Aug. 16, 1847
(Aug. 16, 1847).
John W. Pennington to Tomsey Pennington, Aug. 17, 1847
(Aug. 18, 1847).
James E. Simms to Eliz. M.A. Breckinridge, Aug. 24, 1847
(Aug. 25, 1847).
George W. Meadows to Susan Voss, Aug. 26, 1847 (Aug. 26,
1847).
Franklin Richardson to Mary H. Burkilt, Aug. 31, 1847
(Aug. 31, 1847).
Joshua Green to Arena Gordon, Sept. 2, 1847 (Sept. 2, 1847).
Thomas J. Brice to Mary D. Craig, Sept. 3, 1847 (Sept. 5,
1847).
William Tyler to Janilly A. Moss, Sept. 6, 1847 (Sept. 7,
1847).
Richard M. Long to Sabra P. Ponds, Sept. 10, 1847 (Sept. 14,
1847).
Wm. H. Calloway to Emeline Dalton, Sept. 11, 1847 (Sept. 15,
1847).
William H. Martin to Nancy J. Black, Sept. 13, 1847
(Sept. 14, 1847).
James W. Welch to Mary S. Grissom, Sept. 21, 1847
(Sept. 22, 1847).
John Shields to Malissa Whittington, Sept. 26, 1847
(Sept. 26, 1847).
Starling M. Lindsey to Martha Kelly, Oct. 2, 1847 (Oct. 3,
1847).
Eli H. Bassham to Mariah Finley, Oct. 5, 1847 (Oct. 7,
1847).
Wm. T. Adkisson to Susan Crews, Oct. 5, 1847 (Oct. 7, 1847).
Andrew J. Holland to Susan Taylor, Oct. 6, 1847 (Oct. 7,
1847).
John Tunnage to Mary Ham, Oct. 9, 1847 (Oct. 9, 1847).
Andrew J. Diah to Margaret E. Harder, Oct. 16, 1847
(Oct. 28, 1847).
Philip Manuel to Sara M. Black, Oct. 20, 1847 (Oct. 20,
1847).
Thomas J. Moody to Susannah C. Williams, Oct. 21, 1847.
John A. Gillispie to Harriet M.G. Hooper, Oct. 25, 1847
(Oct. 25, 1847).

Kingston G. Boswell to Mary Ann Wheeler, Nov. 1, 1847 (Nov. 2, 1847).
Wm. F. Blasingame to Jane Spencer, Nov. 3, 1847.
Eli Literal to Mary Ann Cox, Nov. 10, 1847 (Nov. 10, 1847).
Eli Cochran to Carolina Hicks, Nov. 13, 1847 (Nov. 13, 1847).
William L. Parker to Adaline Colier, Nov. 13, 1847.
John Kinnaman to Sarah Gray, Nov. 14, 1847 (Nov. 14, 1847).
Meredith Fulks to Susannah Poteet, Nov. 18, 1847 (Nov. 18, 1847).
Rufus G. Ramsey to Celina Lindsey, Nov. 18, 1847 (Nov. 20, 1847).
Joseph L. Warren to Marcella A. Chaffin, Nov. 20, 1847 (Nov. 21, 1847).
John Eaves to Mary Baker, Nov. 27, 1847 (Nov. 29, 1847).
David D. Reeder to Sarah Jane Stewart, Nov. 27, 1847 (Nov. 30, 1847).
Matthew Jackson to Elizabeth A.E. King, Dec. 1, 1847 (Dec. 2, 1847).
George W. Flippo to Sarah A. Vandiver, Dec. 6, 1847 (Dec. 6, 1847).
Elihu Ingram to Martha Crews, Dec. 8, 1847 (Dec. 8, 1847).
A.G. Osburn to Lucinda McCewen, Dec. 9, 1847 (Dec. 9, 1847).
William Stewart to Anna Benson, Dec. 14, 1847 (Dec. 14, 1847).
Joseph Crews to Susannah Clayton, Dec. 15, 1847.
James Fanning to Emily J. Kirk, Dec. 15, 1847 (Dec. 16, 1847).
B.A. Smith to Nancy Myers, Dec. 18, 1847 (Dec. 19, 1847).
Silas Tipper to Nancy Norwood, Dec. 19, 1847 (Dec. 19, 1847).
Lovin Blasingame to Celia Fisher, Dec. 20, 1847 (Dec. 21, 1847).
Madison Fisher to Telitha Blasingame, Dec. 20, 1847 (Dec. 21, 1847).
Milton McAnally to Synthia H. Pickard, Dec. 23, 1847 (Dec. 23, 1847).
John Gabel to Elvina Quillen, Dec. 24, 1847 (Dec. 28, 1847).
Lewis M. Kirk to Martha Glover, Dec. 28, 1847 (Dec. 28, 1847).
Wm. F. Kirk to Nancy C. White, Dec. 28, 1847 (Dec. 29, 1847).
William M. Hunt to Nancy Richardson, Dec. 28, 1847 (Dec. 28, 1847).
Jackson Poteete to Lorra Hiatt, Dec. 29, 1847 (Dec. 30, 1847).
Riley Shook to Sarah A. White, Dec. 30, 1847 (Dec. 30, 1847).
David Pennington to Rhoda Pennington, Jan. 6, 1848 (Jan. 6, 1848).
George J. Atwell to Cynthia Tripp, Jan. 9, 1848 (Jan. 9, 1848).
James F. Hughes to Eliza A. Jackson, Jan. 13, 1848 (Jan. 13, 1848).

LAWRENCE COUNTY MARRIAGES

Allen J. Atkinson to Lucy Sullivant, Jan. 25, 1848
(Jan. 27, 1848).
Richard Ham to Lucretia Stewart, Jan. 28, 1848 (Jan. 28,
1848).
Eli W. Hollis to Saphronia A. Abritton, Feb. 2, 1848
(Feb. 6, 1848).
John Goode to Delila Izely, Feb. 5, 1848 (Feb. 8, 1848).
Felix Tarkington to Martha Arington, Feb. 13, 1848
(Feb. 13, 1848).
John Harmons to Sarah Neely, Feb. 26, 1848 (Feb. 27, 1848).
Robert Kirk to Margaret Carrell, Mar. 6, 1848 (Mar. 8,
1848).
Giles M. Meek to E.E. Gaither, Mar. 14, 1848 (Mar. 14, 1848).
John Judge to Elizabeth Pierce, Mar. 17, 1848 (Mar. 17,
1848).
John R. Mobley to Nancy C. Hunt, Mar. 18, 1848 (Mar. 19,
1848).
Hiram Morris to Eleanor Lancaster, Mar. 22, 1848 (Mar. 25,
1848).
Daniel Sailors to Elizabeth Moody, Mar. 23, 1848 (Mar. 26,
1848).
George W. Pierce to Lucy Welch, Mar. 23, 1848 (Mar. 23,
1848).
Berry Scott to Elizabeth Scott, Mar. 23, 1848 (Mar. 24,
1848).
James Dial to Elizabeth Gilbert, Mar. 24, 1848 (Mar. 24,
1848).
William Alsup to Elizabeth McMasters, Mar. 25, 1848
(Mar. 28, 1848).
James M. Reddell to Elizabeth Kirk, Mar. 25, 1848 (Mar. 28,
1848).
John McMasters to Nancy Jane Alsup, Mar. 27, 1848 (Mar. 29,
1848).
William Mitchell to Mary Jane Morris, Mar. 27, 1848
(Mar. 27, 1848).
William Glover to Delila Melton, Mar. 9, 1848 (Mar. 9,
1848).
Reuben L. Span to Frances Parkes, Mar. 29, 1848.
Saml H. Bassham to Elizabeth C. Ray, Apr. 20, 1848 (Apr. 20,
1848).
Alfred Hutcheson to Phebe Altum, Apr. 26, 1848 (Apr. 27,
1848).
William Clayton to Lucinda V.O.J. McGree, May 3, 1848
(May 3, 1848).
William Murphy to Jane Powell, May 3, 1848 (May 3, 1848).
Wm. L. Brewington to Nancy Sandy, May 13, 1848 (May 14,
1848).
Jonathan Crews to Elizabeth A. Keelin, May 30, 1848
(June 6, 1848).
Wiley Wammack to Hannah Kilburn, June 21, 1848 (June 22,
1848).
Charles R. McLaren to Catharine Reddell, June 21, 1848
(June 22, 1848).

Robert A. Vorhies to Mary Crostwait, June 22, 1848 (June 23, 1848).
Elias P. Gabel to Levicia Rickman, Apr. 3, 1848 (Apr. 4, 1848).
Thomas E. Kelly to Kary A. Crews, June 28, 1848.
Franklin Ellison to Elizabeth Duncan, June 3, 1848 (June 29, 1848).
William Iseley to Nancy Warren, July 5, 1848 (July 5, 1848).
Edmond H. Kennemer to Mary A. Appleton, July 3, 1848 (July 17, 1848).
John Gilbert to Eliza Ann Futrell, July 7, 1848 (July 7, 1848).
Simon P. Foster to Nancy Crosthwait, July 8, 1848 (July 9, 1848).
George W. Underwood to Frances Lucus, July 8, 1848 (July 8, 1848).
James M. Gibbons to Martha A. Newton, July 12, 1848 (July 13, 1848).
Robert B. Williams to Malinda Branham, July 20, 1848 (July 20, 1848).
M.W. Deavenport to Jane Evans, July 27, 1848 (July 27, 1848).
Joseph Reddell to Eveline Voss, July 29, 1848 (July 30, 1848).
Franklin M. Burris to Charlotte Osburn, July 29, 1848 (July 30, 1848).
Robert Creasy to Anna Davis, Aug. 1, 1848 (Aug. 2, 1848).
Albert J. White to Mariah Scholes, Aug. 22, 1848 (Aug. 24, 1848).
James Bethune to Eliza Patterson, Aug. 29, 1848 (Aug. 30, 1848).
Wm. S. Meadows to Eliz. Ann Davis, Sept. 4, 1848 (Sept. 4, 1848).
Theodore D. Rogers to Eliza J. Shannon, Sept. 14, 1848 (Sept. 19, 1848).
James M. Green to Margaret Osburn, Sept. 16, 1848 (Oct. 12, 1848).
Henry N. Poteet to Nancy McMasters, Sept. 23, 1848 (Oct. 5, 1848).
Bassil Williams to Nancy A. Williams, Sept. 26, 1848 (Sept. 26, 1848).
Alexander Ray to Elizabeth Matthews, Sept. 28, 1848 (Sept. 28, 1848).
Jesse Higgs to Eliz A. Hartless, Sept. 30, 1848 (Oct. 1, 1848).
William Brock to Eveline Gwinn, Oct. 10, 1848 (Oct. 12, 1848).
William Simpson to Sarah Finney, Oct. 11, 1848 (Oct. 11, 1848).
John M. Kilburn to Artimissa R. Parker, Oct. 11, 1848 (Oct. 12, 1848).
Robert L. McLaren to Sarah E. Hale, Oct. 17, 1848 (Oct. 19, 1848).

LAWRENCE COUNTY MARRIAGES

William H. Voss to Martha E. Vorhies, Oct. 21, 1848
(Oct. 22, 1848).
Stephen Stewart to Zilpha Ayres, Oct. 25, 1848 (Oct. 25,
1848).
Hillary Blasingame to Rachael Heffington, Oct. 25, 1848.
John Henry to Christian Atkinson, Nov. 7, 1848 (Nov. 9,
1848).
Jacob French to Nancy Morrison, Nov. 8, 1848 (Nov. 19,
1848).
John E. Brice to Missourie C. Brock, Nov. 15, 1848 (Nov. 16,
1848).
John Kyle to Permelia Reddell, Nov. 18, 1848 (Nov. 18, 1848).
Isaac W. Curtis to Martha Williams, Nov. 27, 1848 (Nov. 28,
1848).
Wm. H. Chesser to Juliann Osburn, Nov. 30, 1848 (Nov. 30,
1848).
William T. Chapman to Martha Dame, Dec. 2, 1848 (Dec. 3,
1848).
Obed Ratliff to Susan Kindrick, Dec. 3, 1848 (Dec. 3, 1848).
Joshua L. Madden to Eleanor J. McDougal, Dec. 4, 1848
(Dec. 6, 1848).
Branson A. Davis to Catharine Grissom, Dec. 7, 1848 (Dec. 12,
1848).
Allen Eaves to Rosannah Rider, Dec. 9, 1848 (Dec. 17, 1848).
Daniel A.G. Trorbaugh to Mary Ann Essary, Dec. 11, 1848
(Dec. 20, 1848).
Daniel McDougal to Chaney Holland, Dec. 16, 1848 (Dec. 19,
1848).
Berry Morison to Delila Smith, Dec. 16, 1848 (Dec. 17, 1848).
James R. Weaver to Frances Barber, Dec. 16, 1848 (Dec. 20,
1848).
Jesse Oakley to Mary Dalton, Dec. 20, 1848 (Dec. 21, 1848).
Jacob S. Jones to Rebecca Rogers, Dec. 20, 1848 (Dec. 21,
1848).
Tyre R. Yates to Hannah McMasters, Dec. 21, 1848 (Dec. 21,
1848).
M.M. Samford to Mary Curry, Dec. 21, 1848 (Dec. 21, 1848).
Charles Moten to Levina Spain, Dec. 23, 1848 (Dec. 24, 1848).
Thomas D. Holland to Catharine E.M. Caskell, Dec. 26, 1848
(Dec. 27, 1848).
Irvine T. Freeman to Nancy L. Hughes, Dec. 26, 1848 (Dec. 26,
1848).
Isaac Pennington to Barbary J. Pennington, Dec. 27, 1848
(Dec. 27, 1848).
James S. Tenneson to Elizabeth L. Curry, Dec. 28, 1848
(Dec. 28, 1848).
George White to Matilda Rogers, Jan. 1, 1849 (Jan. 2, 1849).
Washington L. Cole to Margaret Ann Thompson, Jan. 4, 1849
(Jan. 4, 1849).
Peter Scales to Tennessee Gilmore, Jan. 4, 1849 (Jan. 4,
1849).
Jason W. Boshera to Winney Weaver, Jan. 17, 1849 (Jan. 18,
1849).

LAWRENCE COUNTY MARRIAGES

A.J. Bromley to Martha J. Christian, Jan. 24, 1849
(Jan. 24, 1849).
Ephrain Churchwell to Analiza Floyd, Jan. 29, 1849
(Feb. 1, 1849).
James A. Brewer to Jane Ann Carroll, Jan. 29, 1849
(Jan. 29, 1849).
James Jones to Lavina A. Walker, Jan. 29, 1849 (Jan. 31,
1849).
Wm. P. Thompson to Jane Cole, Feb. 1, 1849 (Feb. 1, 1849).
Martin H. Moody to Parmelia Quillin, Feb. 5, 1849 (Feb. 7,
1849).
A.B. Wisdom to Eliza Chaffin, Feb. 8, 1849 (Feb. 8, 1849).
Demsey Taylor to Mary Tripp, Feb. 13, 1849 (Feb. 13, 1849).
Augustus B. Gordon to Martha Blasingame, Feb. 17, 1849
(Feb. 21, 1849).
Nathaniel Flippo to Telitha Hodge, Mar. 10, 1849 (Mar. 15,
1849).
Robert Chennault to Lucy Ann Vandiver, Mar. 12, 1849
(Mar. 12, 1849).
Augustin Crews to Elizabeth Lindsey, Mar. 17, 1849.
Ira Cutbirth to Jane Floyd, Mar. 19, 1849 (Mar. 25, 1849).
Josiah Evans to Martha M. Curtis, Mar. 22, 1849 (Mar. 24,
1849).
Alexander Lumpkins to Lucinda C. Chapman, Mar. 24, 1849
(Mar. 29, 1849).
Benjamin Crews to Dorcas Lindsey, Apr. 3, 1849 (Apr. 4,
1849).
Elijah Morris to Nancy E. Morris, Apr. 5, 1849 (Apr. 5,
1849).
Ridden B. Owens to Amitha Mallard, Apr. 14, 1849 (Apr. 15,
1849).
John K. Choate to Mahala J. Pollock, Apr. 24, 1849 (Apr. 24,
1849).
Tyrrell Bradley to Lety Eskew, Apr. 24, 1849 (Apr. 24,
1849).
James C. Weaver to Martha Miles, Apr. 26, 1849 (Apr. 26,
1849).
Edward R. Freeman to Cynthia Evans, Apr. 30, 1849 (Apr. 3,
1849).
William Carter to Sarah C. Pollock, May 1, 1849 (May 2,
1849).
Jacob Luttz to Eliz Ferrill, May 7, 1849 (May 7, 1849).
Robert A. Reddell to Sarah Ethridge, May 31, 1849 (May 31,
1849).
William J. Todd to Susannah Clark, June 2, 1849 (June 3,
1849).
John Cross to Sarah Stewart, June 9, 1849 (June 11, 1849).
Wm. Carroll to Anne Scott, June 14, 1849 (June 14, 1849).
Isaiah Hagan to Elizabeth Smith, June 22, 1849 (June 2,
1849).
Henry C. Chambers to Susan Johnson, June 25, 1849 (June 25,
1849).
Edward B. Horne to Tabitha Anne Lindsey, June 26, 1849
(June 26, 1849).

LAWRENCE COUNTY MARRIAGES

Thomas Curtis to Nancy Derveast, July 9, 1849 (July 15, 1849).
John McCarstin to Sophronia E. Tarkington, July 10, 1849 (July 10, 1849).
James L. Stribling to Mary J. Alexander, July 15, 1849 (July 15, 1849).
M.B. Buchanan to Angeline A. Simonton, July 24, 1849 (July 24, 1849).
Henry S. Pickard to Nancy Massey, July 25, 1849 (July 26, 1849).
Ephram McClain to Telia Ann Clendenin, July 28, 1849 (Aug. 2, 1849).
James S. Norwood to Martha Elizabeth Walker, Aug. 2, 1849.
Chapley Smith to Mary Ann Bowman, Aug. 6, 1849 (Aug. 7, 1849).
Andrew C. Vandiver to Sara Sailors, Aug. 7, 1849 (Aug. 7, 1849).
James M. Green to Adaline Belue, Aug. 9, 1849 (Aug. 9, 1849).
John J. Pickard to Eliz M. Pennington, Aug. 10, 1849 (Aug. 12, 1849).
James D. Estes to Mary A.E. Bishop, Aug. 11, 1849 (Aug. 12, 1849).
Wm. H. Blanton to Mary A.R. Mason, Aug. 13, 1849 (Aug. 13, 1849).
Daniel Adkisson to Julina Stewart, Aug. 15, 1849 (Aug. 19, 1849).
Balaam Vaughan to Adaline Curtis, Aug. 16, 1849.
Elihu Altum to Julia A. Roach, Aug. 18, 1849 (Aug. 30, 1849).
Levi Davis to Lucinda Watson, Aug. 21, 1849 (Aug. 22, 1849).
E.W. Manford to Amelia A. Watkins, Aug. 27, 1849.
Enoch Tucker to Margaret A. Rinck, Sept. 3, 1849 (Sept. 13, 1849).
Charles W. Brock to Ruth L. Gwinn, Sept. 7, 1849 (Sept. 7, 1849).
William R. Pace to Sarah Hendrix, Sept. 12, 1849 (Sept. 13, 1849).
John A. Warren to Margaret Ivey, Sept. 18, 1849 (Sept. 19, 1849).
John McGee to Mary Clayton, Sept. 20, 1849 (Aug. 20, 1849).
Alfred Beshers to Margaret J. Orr, Sept. 20, 1849 (Sept. 20, 1849).
Newton M. Gillespie to Ann E. Hooper, Sept. 24, 1849 (Sept. 25, 1849).
Samuel Cox to Nancy C. Hammonds, Oct. 1, 1849 (Oct. 2, 1849).
Spencer C. Dickson to Martha A. Uzzell, Oct. 4, 1849 (Oct. 4, 1849).
Joseph G. Gallaher to Rhoda Lay, Oct. 10, 1849 (Oct. 10, 1849).
Jacob Pennington to Angeline Wilsford, Oct. 13, 1849 (Oct. 14, 1849).

LAWRENCE COUNTY MARRIAGES

Raford F. Pearce to Margaret Broshers, Oct. 16, 1849 (Oct. 19, 1849).
Lewis G. Fields to Nancy M. Johnston, Oct. 22, 1849 (Oct. 23, 1849).
Wm. A. Stewart to Martha Patterson, Oct. 22, 1849 (Oct. 23, 1849).
Clayton B. Luker to Margaret J. Gilmore, Oct. 31, 1849.
Duncan Brice to Nancy G. Turner, Nov. 5, 1849 (Nov. 16, 1849).
Harman Abernathy to Jane Turner, Nov. 8, 1849 (Nov. 13, 1849).
John W. Jeffries to Effa McNeill, Nov. 8, 1849 (Nov. 8, 1849).
George W. Lowrey to Lotty Christian, Nov. 24, 1849.
George C. Lucus to Sophia J. Uzzell, Dec. 2, 1849 (Dec. 2, 1849).
Henry N. Estes to Nancy Kennedy, Dec. 6, 1849 (Dec. 6, 1849).
George W. Carter to Phebe Ann Bennett, Dec. 14, 1849 (Dec. 16, 1849).
George W. Shelton to Elizabeth Johnson, Dec. 19, 1849 (Dec. 18, 1849).
William C. McWhirter to Mary Ann Williams, Dec. 24, 1849 (Dec. 25, 1849).
W.F. Duncan to N.C. McAnally, Dec. 24, 1849 (Dec. 27, 1849).
Thomas Ray to Tabitha Prince, Dec. 26, 1849.
Carroll Tucker to Martha E. Petty, Jan. 1, 1850 (Jan. 1, 1850).
Amos Prater Holland to Mary Jane McKaskil, Jan. 14, 1850 (Jan. 17, 1850).
Reuben Wood to Mary Fuget, Jan. 16, 1850 (Jan. 17, 1850).
Daniel A. Retch to Mary Ann Culbirth, Jan. 20, 1850 (Jan. 20, 1850).
William M. Rose to A.L. Tipton, Jan. 21, 1850 (June 22, 1850).
John L. Reddell to Lucy J. Baker, Jan. 29, 1850 (Jan. 31, 1850).
Moses Moody to Mahala C. Floyd, Jan. 29, 1850 (Jan. 30, 1850).
Wm. Hickman to Elizabeth Coffman, Jan. 30, 1850 (Jan. 30, 1850).
A.O. Richardson to Nancy J. Stephenson, Feb. 2, 1850 (Feb. 3, 1850).
James F. Rogers to Elizabeth Comer, Feb. 5, 1850 (Feb. 5, 1850).
J.F. Wasson to S.R. Kennedy, Feb. 20, 1850 (Feb. 20, 1850).
James F. Cross to Eliza J. Goff, Mar. 4, 1850 (Mar. 24, 1850).
James W. Watson to Sarah Ann Wallace, Mar. 8, 1850 (Mar. 10, 1850).
John H. Marks to Martha E. Tarkington, Mar. 9, 1850 (Mar. 9, 1850).
John B. Underwood to Harriet Pernell, Mar. 21, 1850 (Mar. 23, 1850).
George W. Wilsford to Frances J. Caldwell, Mar. 24, 1850.

LAWRENCE COUNTY MARRIAGES

Richard Polk to Mariah Porter, Mar. 25, 1850 (Mar. 26, 1850).
J.B. Clayton to Elizabeth Crews, Apr. 2, 1850 (Apr. 3, 1850).
Andrew J. Stinnett to Nancy E. McCrackin, Apr. 9, 1850 (Apr. 9, 1850).
Sameul McLean to Susan McLaren, Jan. 8, 1850 (Jan. 8, 1850).
Stephen L. Wood to Martha E. Setters, Apr. 20, 1850 (Apr. 21, 1850).
A.M. Gilespie to Sarah A. McLean, Apr. 20, 1850 (Apr. 21, 1850).
Ira North to Martha Skillern, Apr. 19, 1850.
Reuben Franklin to Margaret J. Gilmon, Apr. 24, 1850 (Apr. 24, 1850).
Wm. W. Anthony to Eliz. Ann Richardson, Apr. 29, 1850 (May 1, 1850).
Benjamin Morris to Matilda Leigh, May 8, 1850 (May 8, 1850).
William Miles to Cynthia Holden, May 15, 1850 (May 15, 1850).
C.C. Hudson to Elizabeth Weaver, May 25, 1850 (May 26, 1850).
Darling M. Tidwell to Roxana W. McCrackin, May 30, 1850.
Clayton B. Luke to Sarah M. Pernell, June 4, 1950 (June 5, 1850).
John B. Underwood to Harriet Pernell, June 9, 1850 (June 9, 1850).
William Kilburn to Mahulda White, June 11, 1850 (June 12, 1850).
Martin C. Abernathy to Sara Calloway, June 15, 1850 (June 16, 1850).
Benjamin F. Brice to Mary J. Spur, June 19, 1850 (June 20, 1850).
Jonathan M. Eaves to Susan Kelly, June 23, 1850 (Sept. 20, 1850).
Elijah Lauderdale to Sarah Spears, June 29, 1850 (June 30, 1850).
John Wilson to Mary A. Simpson, July 9, 1850 (July 9, 1850).
Jesse Trorbaugh to Ruth Essary, July 12, 1850 (July 14, 1850).
Daniel Sullivant to Mary Rockley, July 13, 1850 (July 14, 1850).
Jackson Pace to Mourning Logan, July 18, 1850 (July 18, 1850).
George Ray to Nancy Norman, July 23, 1850 (July 23, 1850).
Thomas McCrory to Elizabeth Potts, Aug. 1, 1850.
Levi Pillow to Eliz Wilcockson, Aug. 1, 1850 (Aug. 1, 1850).
William H. Fogg to Mary Jane Neale, Aug. 1, 1850 (Aug. 1, 1850).
William Cockran to Emeline Heffington, Aug. 10, 1850 (Aug. 14, 1850).
Joseph Anderson to Jane E. Douglass, Aug. 11, 1850 (Aug. 11, 1850).
Willis F. Miles to Martha Ann Estes, Aug. 12, 1850 (Aug. 15, 1850).
George A. Potts to Lucinda McAnally, Aug. 14, 1850.

63

M.V. Bently to H.J. Tarkington, Aug. 16, 1850 (Aug. 18, 1850).

Solomon Wood to Nancy Bassham, Aug. 21, 1850 (Aug. 23, 1850).

Francis M. Wisdom to Mary Chaffin, Aug. 22, 1850 (Aug. 22, 1850).

Calvin Jones to Nancy Simms, Aug. 23, 1850 (Aug. 25, 1850).

John Chisholm to Isabella Campbell, Aug. 25, 1850 (Nov. 17, 1850).

Willis Brown to Elizabeth Osburn, Sept. 2, 1850 (Sept. 2, 1850).

Franklin Davis to Frances M. Norman, Sept. 7, 1850 (Sept. 10, 1850).

Daniel Guthrie to Nancy J. Stribling, Sept. 15, 1850 (Sept. 16, 1850).

John Parker to Emily F. Porter, Sept. 18, 1850 (Sept. 18, 1850).

Sameul C. Morris to Vicey Carrell, Sept. 19, 1850 (Sept. 19, 1850).

Joshua B. Ashmore to Elizabeth Revell, Sept. 21, 1850 (Sept. 22, 1850).

B.H. Allen to M.J. Parkes, Sept. 26, 1850 (Sept. 26, 1850).

James Martin to Eliz. L. Ivey, Sept. 26, 1850 (Sept. 26, 1850).

Jno. B. Tennesson to Hannah C. Norman, Sept. 28, 1850 (Sept. 29, 1850).

Nathan Stockard to Sarah Voss, Sept. 29, 1850.

Wm. H. Kennedy to Sarah A. Davidson, Oct. 1, 1850 (Oct. 1, 1850).

Barton Barnett to Mary J. McGee, Oct. 9, 1850 (Oct. 10, 1850).

Saml F. Murrah to Rachael Harrelson, Oct. 14, 1850 (Oct. 16, 1850).

Jonathan McMasters to Eliza Poteet, Oct. 15, 1850 (Oct. 17, 1850).

Wm. F. Morrow to Louisa J. Wilcockson, Oct. 17, 1850 (Oct. 17, 1850).

James E. Hughes to Martha C. Boswell, Oct. 22, 1850 (Oct. 22, 1850).

Feliz Glover to L.W. Vandiver, Oct. 24, 1850 (Oct. 24, 1850).

Eligy Alsup to Eliza Miller, Oct. 28, 1850 (Oct. 29, 1850).

Moses Cox to Sarah R. McWhirter, Oct. 28, 1850 (Nov. 3, 1850).

John B. Burkilt to Emma E. Springer, Oct. 30, 1850 (Oct. 30, 1850).

John F. Foster to Mary Hooper, Oct. 31, 1850 (Oct. 31, 1850).

Vines H. Cross to Louisa J. Inman, Oct. 30, 1850 (Oct. 31, 1850).

C.K. Rogers to Eliz M. White, Nov. 12, 1850 (Nov. 17, 1850).

James T. Grisham to Anna H. Heffington, Nov. 13, 1850 (Nov. 14, 1850).

LAWRENCE COUNTY MARRIAGES

Wm. Whitworth to Angeline Lindsey, Nov. 14, 1850 (Nov. 14, 1850).
Josiah Jones to Nancy Hamm, Nov. 14, 1850 (Nov. 14, 1850).
Robert J. Bolin to Mary J. Matthews, Nov. 20, 1850 (Nov. 20, 1850).
Thomas G. Scaggs to Nancy Fisher, Nov. 22, 1850 (Nov. 28, 1850).
William Floyd to Nancy C. McNeill, Nov. 13, 1850 (Nov. 24, 1850).
Thomas G. Curry to Martha C. West, Dec. 5, 1850 (Dec. 5, 1850).
James W. Thompson to Josepphine M.C. Brashers, Dec. 9, 1850 (Dec. 12, 1850).
Wm. P. Crabb to Elizabeth Horn, Dec. 11, 1850 (Dec. 12, 1850).
James Chesser to Eliza Blythe, Dec. 11, 1850 (Dec. 11, 1850).
William Reeves to Mary Williams, Dec. 16, 1850 (Dec. 16, 1850).
John Letsinger to Nancy Anthony, Dec. 18, 1850 (Dec. 21, 1850).
A.R. Letner to Frances Burks, Dec. 19, 1850 (Dec. 19, 1850).
Giles H. Cox to Mary Kelsy, Dec. 21, 1850 (Dec. 22, 1850).
Elihu Edmiston to Elvira M.C. Gordon, Dec. 23, 1850 (Dec. 23, 1850).
Daniel J. White to A.V.C. Bassham, Dec. 23, 1850 (Dec. 24, 1850).
Hosea Miles to Cynthia Tripp, Dec. 25, 1850 (Dec. 25, 1850).
Stephen Morrow to Caroline Daniel, Dec. 25, 1850 (Dec. 26, 1850).
Samuel Sullivant to Mary E. Vaughn, Dec. 26, 1850.
William J. Brown to Mahala Busby, Dec. 26, 1850.
Allen Bassham to Eleanor Finley, Dec. 28, 1850 (Dec. 31, 1850).
Merrill Love to Elizabeth Pelt, Dec. 29, 1850 (Dec. 30, 1850).
George W. Lowry to Milly Bradley, Dec. 30, 1850 (Dec. 30, 1850).
Miles M. Green to Julia Harland, Dec. 31, 1850 (Jan. 2, 1851).
George W. Breckinridge to Cyrania J. Chesser, Jan. 1, 1851 (Jan. 1, 1851).
Wm. M. Norman to Sarah Jane McLean, Jan. 4, 1851 (Jan. 7, 1851).
James Griffin to Nancy Randals, Jan. 8, 1851 (Jan. 8, 1851).
Benj. D. Powell to Balzara Bean, Jan. 6, 1851 (Jan. 7, 1851).
Leander McMasters to Martha J. Dobbins, Jan. 6, 1851 (Jan. 12, 1851).
Preston Williams to Manerva Gower, Jan. 9, 1851.
Thos. J. Robertson to Martha Rosser, Jan. 10, 1851 (Jan. 12, 1851).
William L. Ivey to Ann E. Pullen, Jan. 14, 1851 (Jan. 14, 1851).

LAWRENCE COUNTY MARRIAGES

Houston Baker to Charity A. Lewis, Jan. 20, 1851 (Jan. 23, 1851).
Harrison Halland to Ibby Hollis, Jan. 25, 1851 (Jan. 29, 1851).
James Nelson to Susan Green, Jan. 22, 1851 (Jan. 23, 1851).
Joel Williams to Teressa C. Gower, Jan. 28, 1851.
John H. Wall to Susan M. Wisdom, Jan. 28, 1851 (Jan. 30, 1851).
John E. Williams to Sarahan E. Buttler, Feb. 1, 1851 (Feb. 3, 1851).
Joel Davidson to Mary E. Cody, Feb. 3, 1851 (Feb. 4, 1851).
Fountain J. Dixon to Rebecca Gallaher, Feb. 5, 1851 (Feb. 6, 1851).
Eli Cockran to Mary L. Morris, Feb. 13, 1851 (Feb. 14, 1851).
Thomas M. Kelly to Amanda E. White, Feb. 27, 1851 (Feb. 27, 1851).
Robert W. Storry to Elizabeth Barber, Feb. 28, 1851.
John M. Gower to Eliza Williams, Mar. 1, 1851.
Jasper Dueast to Jane Cochran, Mar. 1, 1851 (Mar. 2, 1851).
Eli P. Cooper to Martha Prior, Mar. 4, 1851 (Mar. 4, 1851).
James Eaton to Angeline Ingram, Mar. 5, 1851 (Mar. 5, 1851).
John A. Nichols to Mary H. Kirksey, Mar. 11, 1851 (Mar. 11, 1851).
Zachariah Owens to Sarah J. Massey, Mar. 13, 1851 (Mar. 13, 1851).
Wm. R. Alexander to Sara Thornton, Mar. 22, 1851 (Mar. 23, 1851).
John L. Duckes to Jane Moody, Mar. 25, 1851 (Mar. 27, 1851).
James B. Maxey to Louisa Ivey, Mar. 25, 1851 (Mar. 25, 1851).
James Eskew to Nancy D. Hendrix, Apr. 8, 1851 (Apr. 8, 1851).
Thomas Curry to Sarah Strayhorn, Apr. 12, 1851 (Apr. 14, 1851).
Job Barnett to Nancy Marcum, Apr. 21, 1851 (Apr. 21, 1851).
Jonathan Dalton to Manerva James, Apr. 30, 1851 (May 1, 1851).
George W. Delk to Melita J. Albritton, May 6, 1851 (May 6, 1851).
Wm. C. Roland to Eliza Percy, May 21, 1851 (May 21, 1851).
James Penny to Mary Smith, May 22, 1851 (May 25, 1851).
Albert M. Whitley to Lucinda E. Williams, June 3, 1851 (June 3, 1851).
Jeremiah Berward to Martha J. Gray, June 7, 1851 (June 7, 1851).
Washington Griffin to Mary J. Bassham, June 24, 1851 (June 24, 1851).
James H. Sheppard to Margaret M. Smith, June 24, 1851 (June 24, 1851).
George W. Brewer to Nancy Gordon, June 24, 1851 (June 24, 1851).
William J. Kelly to Rebecca A. Carter, June 24, 1851.
James H. Hardin to Edith Pope, June 25, 1851 (June 25, 1851).
Stephen S. Frazier to Eleanor E. Faust, June 25, 1851 (June 26, 1851).

LAWRENCE COUNTY MARRIAGES

D.B.M. Conway to Nancy Lewis, June 29, 1851 (June 29, 1851).
Joseph M. Dalton to Eliza J. Smith, June 30, 1851.
Wm. J.A. McCaskill to Mary Blasingame, July 2, 1851.
Wm. N. Quillan to Mehala C. McCaskill, July 2, 1851 (July 2, 1851).
W.K.M. Breckenridge to Dice Wilson, July 3, 1851 (July 3, 1851).
Francis M. Green to Louisa W. Smith, July 6, 1851 (July 6, 1851).
Henry S. Smith to Rebecca A. Goodwin, July 7, 1851 (July 13, 1851).
Thomas J. Turnbow to Careline M. Grissom, July 14, 1851 (July 16, 1851).
Nathaniel Mills to Elizabeth Stanford, July 16, 1851 (July 16, 1851).
John M. Carroll to Martha L. Grissom, July 21, 1851 (July 22, 1851).
James M. Dixon to Elizabeth Tucker, July 30, 1851 (July 31, 1851).
John M. Moore to Camilla A. Hall, Aug. 4, 1851 (Aug. 4, 1851).
Jefferson B. Rider to Martha J. Watson, Aug. 14, 1851 (Aug. 14, 1851).
Jeptha Hughes to Elizabeth Allen, Aug. 20, 1851.
John J. Lacroix to Griscilda Olive, Aug. 20, 1851 (Aug. 21, 1851).
Harrison Ons to Nancy Ons, Aug. 21, 1851 (Aug. 21, 1851).
James Hooper to Margaret Sprinkles, Aug. 26, 1851 (Sept. 20, 1851).
Jesse Renfro to Ticey McQuigg, Sept. 1, 1851 (Sept. 9, 1851).
Aaron Foust to Eliz Ann Dobbins, Sept. 13, 1851 (Sept. 14, 1851).
Alfred Lunn to Mary J. Norwood, Sept. 15, 1851 (Sept. 15, 1851).
Wm. B. White to Susan Hardiman, Sept. 15, 1851 (Sept. 16, 1851).
Francis M. Rose to Mary S. Rea, Sept. 15, 1851 (Sept. 30, 1851).
Calvin A. Powell to Mary J. Hammonds, Sept. 19, 1851 (Sept. 24, 1851).
Joel J. Foster to Nancy Ratliff, Sept. 30, 1851 (Sept. 30, 1851).
Wm. A. Pillow to Eupphene Meadows, Sept. 30, 1851 (Sept. 30, 1851).
Wm. S. Morrow to Manerva J. Foster, Oct. 10, 1851 (Oct. 12, 1851).
Matthew G. Russ to Lavonia A. Dickson, Oct. 15, 1851 (Oct. 15, 1851).
James V. Willis to Adaline Williams, Oct. 15, 1851 (Oct. 16, 1851).
John Yancy to Tennessee Story, Oct. 15, 1851 (Oct. 16, 1851).
Thomas Blasingame to Mary Canada, Oct. 16, 1851.

Andrew M. Lathem to Manerva A. Foster, Oct. 16, 1851
(Oct. 16, 1851).
Albert J.M. White to Louisa Voss, Oct. 21, 1851 (Oct. 22,
1851).
John W. Austin to Ruth Ann Klyce, Oct. 22, 1851 (Oct. 23,
1851).
Jacob Campbell to Margaret Belew, Oct. 25, 1851 (Oct. 28,
1851).
William T. Neale to Semantha T. Lindsey, Oct. 25, 1851
(Oct. 26, 1851).
James A. Nevill to A.V.B. High, Nov. 9, 1851 (Nov. 9, 1851).
David H. White to Milley Jane Roper, Nov. 10, 1851 (Nov. 12,
1851).
Willis Brewington to Sarah Garner, Nov. 11, 1851 (Nov. 12,
1851).
George Potete to Sarah Barber, Nov. 12, 1851 (Nov. 13, 1851).
James C. Morrison to Mary J. Barnet, Nov. 17, 1851 (Nov. 27,
1851).
Ananias Wilbourn to Ruth J. Springer, Nov. 18, 1851
(Nov. 20, 1851).
Abraham Pennington to Elmira McAnally, Nov. 18, 1851
(Nov. 23, 1851).
James Pearce to Sarah A. Greenhaw, Nov. 20, 1851 (Nov. 20,
1851).
Franklin Cavin to Suson Watson, Nov. 24, 1851 (Nov. 24,
1851).
Thomas Mitchell to Sarah Jane Barnes, Nov. 24, 1851.
Charles D. Hale to A.J.E. Webb, Dec. 3, 1851 (Dec. 3, 1851).
Wm. S. Rickets to Lucy Pickard, Dec. 2, 1851 (Dec. 3, 1851).
Reuben Lovell to Martha Cottrell, Dec. 10, 1851 (Dec. 10.
1851).
Lennuel A. Ezell to Martha Comer, Dec. 24, 1851 (Dec. 25,
1851).
James Williams to Catharine Hill, Dec. 26, 1851 (Dec. 26,
1852).
Thomas M. McBride to Sarah E. Jones, Dec. 27, 1851 (Dec. 28,
1851).
Claborn Palmore to Hannah Jackson, Dec. 29, 1851 (Dec. 30,
1851).
John E. Hatcher to Mary E. McKnight, Dec. 30, 1851 (Dec. 30,
1851).
Josiah J. Galloway to Mary J. Chambers, Jan. 1, 1851
(Jan. 1, 1851).
Isaac L. Sullivant to Ethelinda Burney, Jan. 1, 1851
(Jan. 1, 1851).
Wm. A. Stewart to Adaline Lay, Jan. 3, 1851 (Jan. 4, 1851).
William N. Hensley to Sarah A. Bailey, Jan. 10, 1852
(Jan. 17, 1852).
Ferdinan F. Joyce to Elizabeth Clayton, Jan. 14, 1852
(Jan. 14, 1852).
John McMasters to Manerva J. Miller, Jan. 26, 1852
(Jan. 26, 1852).
James Burnes to Eliza A. Pollock, Jan. 27, 1852 (Jan. 26,
1852).

LAWRENCE COUNTY MARRIAGES

John H. Rickman to Emily Mires, Jan. 27, 1852 (Jan. 27, 1852).
James Nipper to Rebecca Younger, Feb. 5, 1852 (Feb. 5, 1852).
Francis M. Frank to Manerva J. McClendon, Feb. 13, 1852 (Feb. 15, 1852).
Samuel Weaver to Eliz E. Duckworth, Feb. 17, 1852 (Feb. 17, 1852).
James H. Albritton to Elizabeth Crews, Feb. 24, 1852 (Feb. 26, 1852).
Cleborn Bundrant to Mary Ann Crews, Mar. 1, 1852.
Daniel Voss to Mary J. Cook, Mar. 6, 1852 (Mar. 7, 1852).
Francis M. Oliver to Catharine Foster, Mar. 15, 1852 (Mar. 27, 1852).
Wm. J. Pennington to Saphronia Williams, Mar. 18, 1852 (Mar. 18, 1852).
Charles Quillen to Mary Bundrant, Mar. 20, 1852.
David Hughes to Jane Smith, Mar. 27, 1852 (Mar. 28, 1852).
King Kinbrell to Nancy Redden, Apr. 5, 1852.
Wm. T. Bryant to Hannah E. Lindsey, Apr. 6, 1852.
John Bassham to Elizabeth Roper, Nov. 3, 1852 (Nov. 6, 1852).
James H. Gilespie to Elizabeth L. McMillan, Apr. 26, 1852 (Apr. 26, 1852).
Alexander Williams to Jane Whitworth, Apr. 28, 1852 (Apr. 29, 1852).
Nicholas Terry to Mary Ann McClure, May 15, 1852.
James B. Harrison to Laurey A. Gibbins, May 20, 1852.
Thomas B. Smith to Mary A. Norman, Oct. 13, 1851 (Oct. 19, 1851).
Hilliard Harmon to D.B.B. Pryor, May 23, 1852 (May 23, 1852).
Nicholas Spears to Sarah Jane Griggs, May 27, 1852 (May 27, 1852).
S.P. Watson to Rebecca Bray, May 29, 1852 (May 30, 1852).
William McCutchen to Deanah Myers, June 8, 1852 (June 8, 1852).
G.W.H. Nowlin to Lucy J. Nowlin, June 10, 1852 (June 10, 1852).
Moses Wright to Manerva J. Turner, June 14, 1852 (June 14, 1852).
Samuel Putman to Mary Ann Call, June 21, 1852 (June 21, 1852).
Thos. A. McDonald to Sarah A. Atkisson, June 24, 1852 (June 24, 1852).
Thomas C. Defoe to Sarah Ann Norwood, July 1, 1852 (July 1, 1852).
J.S. Clayton to Rachel Curtis, July 3, 1852 (July 8, 1852).
Weakley G. Kennedy to Sarah A. Stockard, July 7, 1852 (July 7, 1852).
John Morrow to Elizabeth J. Curtis, July 8, 1852.
John P. McNeill to Mary F. Dame, July 17, 1852 (July 18, 1852).
John W. Stewart to Martha Blair, July 19, 1852 (July 22, 1852).

LAWRENCE COUNTY MARRIAGES

J.K. Spears to Elizabeth J. Dishough, July 31, 1852
(Aug. 1, 1852).
William Ezell to Nancy Mary Ann Ezell, Aug. 11, 1852
(Aug. 12, 1852).
John Judge to Rachel Cockran, Aug. 17, 1852 (Aug. 19, 1852).
James A. Short to Rosannah Eaves, Aug. 26, 1852
(Aug. 26, 1852).
Benjamin Beard to Sarah P. Andrews, Aug. 30, 1852
(Sept. 3, 1852).
Calvin Spears to Rebecca E. Ramsey, Sept. 7, 1852.
Elijah Smith to Sarah E. Franks, Sept. 8, 1852 (Sept. 9,
1852).
Abner Johnson to Martha Wright, Sept. 8, 1852 (Sept. 8,
1852).
William Springer to Martha J. Smith, Sept. 9, 1852
(Sept. 16, 1852).
Jesse Wall to Nancy E. Rea, Sept. 22, 1852 (Sept. 23,
1852).
William P. Rickard to D.J. Williams, Sept. 23, 1852
(Sept. 23, 1852).
W.P.H. Turner to Manerva McAnally, Sept. 23, 1852
(Sept. 23, 1852).
Thomas G. Cunningham to Sarah J. McLaren, Sept. 27, 1852
(Sept. 28, 1852).
Thomas H. Laxey to Narcissa Yarbough, Oct. 1, 1852.
Daniel K. McGee to Mary J. Crews, Oct. 7, 1852 (Oct. 7,
1852).
B.M. Patteson to Myranda Smith, Oct. 8, 1852 (Oct. 12, 1852).
James Huggins to Nancy A. Pennington, Oct. 12, 1852
(Oct. 12, 1852).
Lewis M. Kirk to Ann Green, Oct. 16, 1852 (Oct. 17, 1852).
Robert W. Appleton to Melissa A. Hammonds, Oct. 23, 1852
(Oct. 24, 1852).
Wm. E. Newton to Rutha Belew, Oct. 25, 1852 (Oct. 26, 1852).
Wm. M. Tesseson to Mary J. Wasson, Oct. 30, 1852
(Oct. 30, 1852).
Wm. D. Moody to Mary A. Brown, Nov. 9, 1852 (Nov. 14, 1852).
Jeffrey Murrell to Mary T. Matthews, Nov. 20, 1852
(Nov. 21, 1852).
Columbus F. Dixon to Sara Ann Springer, Nov. 24, 1852
(Nov. 27, 1852).
Jno. W. Welch to Elizabeth A. McMackin, Dec. 4, 1852
(Dec. 5, 1852).
James M. White to Martha Welch, Dec. 4, 1852 (Dec. 5, 1852).
John Boshers to Nancy H. Billingsly, Dec. 4, 1852
(Dec. 5, 1852).
Thomas Voorhies to Eliza J. Nichols, Dec. 8, 1852 (Dec. 9,
1852).
Robert Dickey to Lucy Kirk, Dec. 14, 1852 (Dec. 15, 1852).
E.B. Wilson to Mary Jane Johnson, Dec. 18, 1852
(Dec. 18, 1852).
Henry S. Pickard to Eliza J. Pennington, Dec. 18, 1852
(Dec. 19, 1852).
W.G. McCafferty to Katharine Newton, Dec. 20, 1852
(Dec. 23, 1852).

Wesley D. Henson to Francis D. Head, Dec. 23, 1852
(Dec. 23, 1852).
Cannon Buttler to Juliann Holtsford, Dec. 23, 1852
(Dec. 23, 1852).
Tobias A. Whitehead to Martha Franklin, Dec. 28, 1852
(Dec. 29, 1852).
Wiley Voss to Mary V. Billinsly, Dec. 28, 1852.
Stephen A. McMackin to Mary Welch, Dec. 30, 1852
(Dec. 30, 1852).
William C. Davis to Tennessee M. Anthony, Dec. 30, 1852
(Dec. 30, 1852).
J.D. Massey to Elizabeth Ann Voss, Jan. 5, 1853 (Jan. 6,
1853).
Zachariah E. Gordon to Soloma G.M. Taylor, Jan. 20, 1853.
Milton Bently to Isabella B. Balch, Jan. 22, 1853
(Jan. 23, 1853).
Alexander Pollock to Amanda L. Collins, Jan. 25, 1853
(Jan. 27, 1853).
Jesse Hughs to Winney A. Green, Feb. 1, 1853 (Feb. 1, 1853).
Perrin Wright to Sarah M. Richardson, Feb. 2, 1853
(Feb. 3, 1853).
Wm. Liles to America Weaver, Feb. 5, 1853 (Feb. 6, 1853).
John E. Williams to Mary Hicks, Feb. 5, 1853 (Feb. 6, 1853).
John Green to Lucy Goad, Feb. 7, 1853 (Feb. 14, 1853).
W.E. Bell to Mary E. Huggins, Feb. 9, 1853 (Feb. 9, 1853).
Ira D. White to Sarah Jane Wilburn, Feb. 14, 1853.
A.B. Smith to Mary J. Bailey, Feb. 15, 1853 (Feb. 15, 1853).
Henry Luceeys to Hannah A. Pryer, Feb. 19, 1853 (Feb. 19,
1853).
William H. Goad to Sarah J. Wilburn, Feb. 21, 1853
(Feb. 21, 1853).
John W. Floyd to Mary H. Shaw, Feb. 23, 1853 (Feb. 27, 1853).
Joseph A. Morrison to Marjoh E. Floyd, Feb. 25, 1853
(Feb. 27, 1853).
Samuel C. Simpson to Louisa Davis, Feb. 25, 1853.
M.B. Rogers to Sarah Jones, Feb. 25, 1853 (Feb. 25, 1853).
Hasten Spears to Amanda Fenney, Feb. 26, 1853 (Feb. 26,
1853).
Robert Nelson to Isabela White, Feb. 26, 1853 (Feb. 27,
1853).
Luke Lee to Sarah C. Carter, Feb. 26, 1853 (Feb. 28, 1853).
James F. Rhods to Sarah D. Gordon, Mar. 5, 1853.
Elias Franklin to Adaline Helton, Mar. 9, 1853 (Mar. 11,
1853).
Henry Finney to Evaline Spears, Mar. 16, 1853 (Mar. 16,
1853).
Matthew Weaver to Sophiah Ervin, Apr. 1, 1853 (Apr. 1, 1853).
James C.R. Williams to Mary Webb, Apr. 5, 1853 (Apr. 7, 1853).
Thomas Brewer to Lucinda C. Staggs, Apr. 6, 1853
(Apr. 8, 1853).
E.J. Blake to Louisa A. Samford, Apr. 7, 1853 (Apr. 8, 1853).
Elisha C. Pollock to Martha J. Austin, Apr. 7, 1853
(Apr. 8, 1853).
R.F. Peare to Elvira M. Hillhouse, Apr. 9, 1853
(Apr. 10, 1853).

Patrick Corcoran to Emeline Alley, Apr. 16, 1853.
John M. Hutcheson to Mary L. Layton, Apr. 18, 1853
  (Apr. 21, 1853).
Granville Cockrell to Dicy Tooten, Apr. 21, 1853
  (Apr. 21, 1853).
James E. Gabel to Nancy M. Stewart, May 9, 1853
  (May 10, 1853).
David Ham to Lucretia J. Cookrell, May 13, 1853
  (May 13, 1853).
James McDanell to Catharine Davis, May 13, 1853
  (May 14, 1853).
Edward Winters to Alsey Mobley, May 25, 1853 (May 25, 1853).
Daniel Patterson to Almiranda A. Breckenridge, June 9,
  1853 (June 9, 1853).
Dennis Belew to Martha Prier, June 18, 1853 (June 18, 1853).
Jonithan Lewis to Winney C. Mitchell, June 23, 1853
  (June 23, 1853).
A.N. Whitley to Lucinda Vails, June 25, 1853 (June 26, 1853).
James J. White to Elener Franklin, June 28, 1853
  (June 29, 1853).
Aaron C. Speer to America H. Speer, July 2, 1853.
L.M. Alley to Eliza A. Read, July 7, 1853 (July 7, 1853).
A.W. Richardson to Mary Estes, July 22, 1853.
Daniel W. May to Martha A. Black, July 22, 1853.
James Randolph to Margrett M. Inmon, July 22, 1853
  (July 22, 1853).
Samuel Blake to Elizabeth Ham, July 24, 1853 (July 24, 1853).
Johnathan Howell to Elizabeth P. Spencer, July 25, 1853
  (July 28, 1853).
Wm. E. Austin to Mary E. Newgent, July 23, 1853
  (July 26, 1853).
Thomas West to Margaret E. Wasson, Aug. 1, 1853 (Aug. 4,
  1853).
William Boswell to Vernettie Green, Aug. 4, 1853
  (Aug 21, 1853).
William F. Hail to Mary Ann Vaughn, Aug. 15, 1853.
Gabriel B. Long to Susan K. Stricklin, Aug. 17, 1853
  (Aug. 18, 1853).
Moses Davis to Vina M. Fugat, Aug. 24, 1853 (Aug. 24, 1853).
Thomas V. Cross to Ibby Ferrill, Aug. 25, 1853 (Aug. 25,
  1853).
John G. Gelison to Sarah A. Kennedy, Aug. 30, 1853
  (Aug. 31, 1853).
John F. Abernathy to Emily E. Richey, Sept. 1, 1853
  (Sept. 1, 1853).
A.J. Linum to Mary Ann Bowden, Sept. 1, 1853 (Sept. 1, 1853).
Harrison Blair to Eliza Jane Scott, Sept. 1, 1853
  (Sept. 1, 1853).
Daniel L. Kelly to Manerva Crews, Sept. 2, 1853 (Sept. 3,
  1853).
Stephen D. Pillow to Mary J. Williams, Sept. 5, 1853
  (Sept. 15, 1853).
Michael Garrett to Ann M. Richey, Sept. 5, 1853
  (Sept. 5, 1853).

LAWRENCE COUNTY MARRIAGES

Seburn Littrell to Sarah Jane Shook, Sept. 5, 1853
(Sept. 8, 1853).
Isaac H. Gobble to Mary Ann Clay, Sept. 5, 1853.
William F. Gower to Elizabeth Bumpass, Sept. 7, 1853
(Sept. 7, 1853).
James H. Lawrence to Margaret E. Anderson, Sept. 13, 1853
(Sept. 13, 1853).
Elias Jones to Louisa Jane Carrell, Sept. 15, 1853
(Sept. 15, 1853).
James M. Anderson to Martha J. Kelton, Sept. 20, 1853
(Sept. 20, 1853).
William Tripp to Sarah Harland, Sept. 22, 1853 (Sept. 22,
1853).
John Miller to Esther Alsup, Sept. 23, 1853 (Sept. 25,
1853).
Robert Cochran to Martha Ann Pollock, Sept. 27, 1853
(Sept. 28, 1853).
Nathan Lamay to Julia Trobough, Sept. 29, 1853 (Sept. 30,
1854).
John B. Rea to Francis Richardson, Oct. 4, 1853 (Oct. 4,
1853).
Thomas J. Shackleford to Mary Ann Boswell, Oct. 5, 1853
(Oct. 6, 1853).
Joseph C. Inman to Elvina J. McAlester, Oct. 10, 1853
(Oct. 13, 1853).
Jasper N. Hollis to Ruthey E. Springer, Oct. 11, 1853
(Oct. 13, 1853).
William H. Bradley to Nancy Burdrant, Oct. 13, 1853.
Stephen S. Frazier to Martha Palmer, Oct. 13, 1853
(Oct. 25, 1853).
P.M. Wright to Martha E. Voss, Oct. 13, 1853 (Oct. 16,
1853).
William Martin to Elizabeth Ann May, Oct. 18, 1853
(Oct. 18, 1853).
Labern Prince to Mahala J. Ray, Oct. 20, 1853 (Oct. 20,
1853).
Isaac N. Spencer to Lucey Ann Wilks, Oct. 21, 1853
(Oct. 23, 1853).
John W. Bradley to Mary E. Ingram, Oct. 22, 1853
(Oct. 23, 1853).
William S. Tharp to Sarah Kelsey, Oct. 24, 1853 (Oct. 26,
1853).
Reubin Franklin to Nancy Jane Roach, Oct. 26, 1853
(Oct. 27, 1853).
Thomas W. Crabb to Rachael E. Nutt, Oct. 27, 1853
(Oct. 27, 1853).
Isaac H. Cobble to Eliza Jane Murphey, Nov. 2, 1853
(Nov. 6, 1853).
James C. Beard to Rebecca Voss, Nov. 5, 1853 (Nov. 6,
1853).
Archibald M. Blue to Elizabeth R. Branch, Nov. 5, 1853
(Nov. 5, 1853).
Thomas J. Pennington to Margaret R. Wood, Nov. 12, 1853
(Nov. 15, 1853).

LAWRENCE COUNTY MARRIAGES

E.W. Tucker to Mary A. McCrory, Nov. 16, 1853 (Nov. 17, 1853).
D.N. Pennington to Caroline Anthony, Nov. 16, 1853 (Nov. 17, 1853).
Wm. B. Williams to Martha E. Pullen, Nov. 21, 1853 (Nov. 21, 1853).
Theodore Clendennon to Drucillah Pope, Nov. 21, 1853 (Nov. 20, 1853).
Nathaniel Flippo to Lucy Jane White, Nov. 26, 1853 (Nov. 27, 1853).
Phillip T.B. Nowlin to Martha H.E. Kidd, Nov. 28, 1853 (Dec. 1, 1853).
James T. Coker to Elizabeth Frances Ray, Nov. 30, 1853 (Nov. 4, 1853).
Anderson Horn to Elizabeth Ann Crabb, Dec. 1, 1853 (Dec. 1, 1853).
Martin H. Smith to Nancy P. Pharr, Dec. 10, 1853.
G.W. O'Bryant to L.A. Brown, Dec. 16, 1853 (Dec. 18, 1853).
Henry Brewington to Elizabeth J. Sanders, Dec. 20, 1853 (Dec. 20, 1853).
Thomas Favour to Nancy J. Downes, Dec. 21, 1853 (Dec. 21, 1853).
Robert T. Cooper to L.C. Smith, Dec. 22, 1853 (Dec. 22, 1853).
Jonathan Eaves to Elizabeth Thompson, Dec. 22, 1853 (Dec. 23, 1853).
Martin Green to Lucinda Miles, Dec. 27, 1853 (Dec. 27, 1853).
James H. King to Martha E. Pennington, Dec. 31, 1853 (Dec. 31, 1853).
James Dame to Mary Ann Voss, Jan. 1, 1854 (Jan. 1, 1854).
Ozias D. Webb to Elizabeth B. Tucker, Jan. 4, 1854 (Jan. 4, 1854).
J.L. Reddell to Sarah A. Martin, Jan. 5, 1854 (Jan. 5, 1854).
James C. Staggs to Sarah J. White, Jan. 5, 1854.
P.B. Vandiver to Ann Boaz, Jan. 9, 1854 (Jan. 10, 1854).
James McClannahan to Elizabeth A. Morrison, Jan. 10, 1854 (Jan. 10, 1854).
Charles T. Brown to Elizabeth Ann Vick, Jan. 12, 1854 (Jan. 12, 1854).
Eli Bell to Elizabeth J. Anthony, Jan. 12, 1854 (Jan. 13, 1854).
John W. Hodges to Sarah Bell, Jan. 12, 1854 (Jan. 13, 1854).
J.S. Brilton to A.R. McBride, Jan. 13, 1854 (Jan. 15, 1854).
John W. Blair to Nancy Hannah, Jan. 14, 1854 (Jan. 15, 1854).
David L. McClamock to Martha Lad, Jan. 16, 1854 (Jan. 16, 1854).
A.J. Powell to Malinda Welch, Jan. 19, 1854 (Jan. 24, 1854).
Joseph Anderson to Nancy Bowie, Jan. 23, 1854 (Jan. 24, 1854).

M.P.R. Branch to Martha J. Williams, Jan. 24, 1854
(Jan. 28, 1854).
John N. Craig to Louisa H. Gwinn, Jan. 28, 1854 (Jan. 29,
1854).

INDEX

Appleton (cont)
Robert W. 70
Archer, Daniel 10
Elizabeth 7
Merrill 2
Nancy 10
Polly 4
Rebecca 3
Arington, Araminta T. 40
Martha 57
Armstrong, Alexander 15
Elizabeth 46
Numinty 23
Arnold, Edward 19, 33
Mary 17
Sarah 19
Winston 53
Asbell, Martha 15
Ashmore, Athalinda 8
Jasindia 31
Joshua B. 44, 64
Askew, Sally 22
Atkinson, Allen J. 57
Christian 59
D. P. 37
Atkisson, Sarah A. 69
Atwell, George J. 56
Nancy 39
Austin, John W. 68
Mahala 46
Martha J. 71
Philip G. 49
William 38
Wm. E. 72
Ayres, Zilpha 57
Badchell, Lizza 13
Bailey, A. B. 7
Booker 50
Edmund 6
J. H. 2
John M. 43
Joseph 46
Joseph E. 49
Louisa V. 49
Mariah 53
Mary J. 71
R. T. 8, 25
Solinah 18
Sarah A. 12
Baily, George 35
Baker, Houston 66
John L. 45
Lucy J. 62
Mary 56

Baker (cont)
Micager 22
Nancy 18
Sarah 14
Thomas 14, 23, 25
William 37
Balch, Isabella B. 71
Ball, Daniel M. 45
Elizabeth 44
William B. 47
Ballard, Barbary 53
Banswell, Kingston G. 43
Barbee, Hiliary W. 14
Nancy F. 14
Barber, Elizabeth 66
Frances 59
Joshua 3
Sarah 68
Barin, Joseph 53
Barner, John W. 46
Barnes, Robert E. 47
Sarah Jane 68
Wm. C. 51
Barnet, Jesse 38
Mary J. 68
Barnett, Barton 64
Elizabeth 44
Ephraim 3
George 36, 38
James W. 42
Jane 51
Job 66
Patsey 5
Barns, Mary 42
Barr, Isaac G. 61
Nathan 10
Basham, Eliz. A. 46
Frances F. 39
J. 38
Marry M. 36
Saml H. 45
T. M. 38
William F. 46
Bashears, Emarilla 36
Henry 38
Nancy 35
Philip F. 53
Bassham, A. V. C. 65
Allen 65
Eli H. 55
James M. 50
John 69
Malinda 24
Mary 4

Bassham (cont)
 Mary J. 66
 Mary M. 32
 Nancy 17, 64
 Nathan 14, 28
 S. D. 43
 Saml H. 57
 Samuel H. 42
Baswell, Burley W. 37
Bateman, Levi H. 53
 R. C. E. 38
 William 39
Baucum, Cader 41
Bean, Balzara 65
 Burthena 8
Beard, Archaday 53
 Benjamin 70
 James C. 73
Beasley, Nancy 32
Beaths, John 46
Beatty, Leticia 26
Beedle, Leticia 11
Beeler, Catharine 19
 William W. 25
Belew, Dennis 72
 Eliza 33
 Jacob 28
 James E. 38
 Jesse 15
 Margaret 68
 Rutha 70
 Ruthey 28
 Zachariah 52
Bell, Cyrus 7, 9
 Eli 74
 Elizabeth 4
 James 37
 John 36, 54
 John J. 29
 Robt. N. 8
 Sally 25
 Sarah 74
 Virginia 19
 W. E. 71
 W. R. 36
Bellew, Nanny 36
Belue, Adaline 61
Bennet, E. J. 41
Bennett, James K. 38
 Phebe Ann 62
Benson, Anna 56
Bentley, John 40
 L. Mine 40
Bently, Leonidas 51

Bently (cont)
 M. V. 64
 Milton 71
Berward, Jeremiah 66
Beshers, Alfred 61
Best, William C. 50
Bethune, James 58
Bevers, Spencer A. 51
Bilew, Susannah 40
Billingsley, Nancy H. 70
 Ruthy 19
Billinsly, Mary V. 71
Bingham, Nancy 52
 Sarah 48
Birch, Agnes Jane 54
Bird, Alford 4
 Holman 53
 Jacob 6, 23
 Polly 2
Birdsong, Miles 15
Birum, Mary 7
Bishop, Joseph 49
 Mary A. E. 61
 Wiley B. 43
Bivens, Juliann 44
Bivins, Emelin 41
Black, Martha A. 22
 Maryan 37
 Nancy J. 55
 Sara M. 55
Blackard, Miry E. 29
Blair, Elizabeth Jane 45
 Harrison 72
 John W. 74
 Martha 69
 Sarah 48
 Wm. C. 50
Blake, E. J. 71
 Samuel 72
Blanton, Wm. H. 61
Blasenfim, Charity 44
Blasengame, L. 38
Blasengim, Thomas C. 44
Blasingam, N. H. 39
Blasingame, Eliza 50
 Hillary 59
 Jacob H. 15
 Lena 40
 Lovin 56
 Martha 60
 Mary 67
 Susan M. 40
 Telitha 56
 Thomas 67

Blasingame (cont)
Wm. F. 56
Blue, Archibald M. 73
  Archibald W. 6
Blyth, Jesse 42
Blythe, Eliza 65
  Elizabeth 13, 36
  Jane 50
  Lemuel 9
  Polly 26
Boaz, Ann 74
Boaze, William 43
Bolen, Silvester 44
Bolin, Robert J. 65
Boshears, Easter 37
  Lucinda J. 44
Boshera, Jason W. 59
Boshers, John 70
Boshiers, Christiana 1
Bossham, Wm. D. 37
Boswell, Burley W. 36
  Elizabeth 11
  Kingston G. 56
  Levi 12
  Martha C. 64
  Mary Ann 73
  Susannah M. 16
  William 72
  Wm. 37
Bowden, Anna 7
  Charles W. 17
  Jackson K. 4
  Loucinda 38
  Lucinda 36
  Mary Ann 72
  Wiley F. 36, 37
  William 4
Bowdon, N. E. 37
Bowdry, Joshua 19
Bowie, Nancy 74
Bowling, Alexr. 40
Bowman, Mary Ann 61
Bradley, Betsey 30
  John W. 73
  Joseph R. 53
  Milly 65
  Rebecca 23
  Richard J. 44
  Tyrrell 60
  W. G. 38
  William H. 73
Bradly, Elisha 39
  Sam 39
Bradshaw, Sarah 32

Bramlett, Sanford 26
Branch, Elizabeth R. 73
  M. P. R. 75
  Susannah G. 45
Branham, Malinda 58
Brashears, Alexander 3, 27
  Anny 28
  Basil 4
  Berry 6
  Henry 19
  Jacob 11, 27
  Jane 23, 26
  Lucinda 6
  Mary 19
  Nancy 3
  Nathan 4
  Nelly 24
  Peter 3
  Polly 15, 21
  Rebecca 3
  Sally 30
  Sarah 17
  Susannah 27
  Walter 4
Brashers, Dicey 53
  Elizath 45
  Josepphine M. C. 65
  Lucinda 39
  Martha Martila 53
Brasier, Samuel 50
Brasures, Jessee 44
Bray, Rebecca 69
Brazhears, Bicy 4
Brazier, Adam 3
Breckenridge, Almiranda A.
  72
  Eliz. M. A. 55
  George W. 65
  James M. 53
  W. K. M. 67
Brewer, George 35
  George W. 66
  James A. 60
  James M. 52
  John J. 52
  John M. 35
  Solomon 37
  Thomas 72
Brewington, Henry 74
  Willis 68
  Wm. L. 57
Brice, Benjamin F. 63
  Duncan 62
  John E. 45, 59

Brice (cont)
Thomas J. 55
Bride, Hugh 44
Briley, Melvina 43
Brilton, J. S. 74
Broadstreet, Wm. 36
Brock, Charles W. 61
Missourie C. 59
William 58
Bromley, A. J. 60
Elizabeth 48
Brooks, James 27
Mary Ann 18
Nancy 9
Broshers, Ethamalinda 40
Margaret 62
Sarah Jane 50
Brown, Charles T. 74
E. J. 44
Eliza 24, 25, 36
Emily 37
George A. 48
Hezekiah 47
John F. 35
L. A. 79
Martha 43
Mary A. 70
Pelina 25, 31, 35
Samuel 7
William 53
William J. 65
Willis 64
Brownlow, Elvire 5
Bruce, Ann R. 55
Jesse M. 54
Brumley, Albert 28
Anna 10
Burrell 29
Cyntha 45
Larkin 5
William 27
Brumly, James 39
Jesse 35
Bryan, Allen H. 44
Jacob 5
Nancy 51
Bryant, Elizabeth 18
Thos. 39
Wm. T. 69
Buchanan, Eleanor 5
Evelina 27
F. 4
Franklin 1, 22
Lucy Ann 47

Buchanan (cont)
M. B. 61
W. T. 46
Buchanon, Marcella 45
Buckitt, James B. 49
Buford, Jane 7
Buie, Daniel 2
Duncan 8, 31, 33
Bullidge, Jane 9
Bumpass, A. W. 9, 29
Alsey 6
Elizabeth 73
Emily 28
Ethelina L. 39
Frances D. 48
Gabe 38
H. C. 37
J. M. 23
James M. 3
James W. 44
Marian 13
Sophia 29
Bundrant, Cleborn 69
Mary 69
Bunpass, Marian 13
Burdrant, Nancy 73
Burgess, Henderson 52
Burke, Anney 20
Burkes, Raiford 51
Burket, Lavine 17
Lucy C. 35
Nancy 9
Wm. 9
Burkett, Jane 25
Burkilt, John B. 64
Mary H. 55
Burkit, Lucy C. 26
Burks, Claburn 35
Frances 65
Burlison, Celia 5
Burliston, Ann 28
Burlow, William 49
Burman, Elizabeth 23
Burnes, James 68
Burnet, Katy 16
Burney, Charles J. 50
Ethelinda 68
Burns, Berryman 28
Emily 24
Israel 24
James 5
Samuel 38
Burris, Franklin M. 58
John 1, 29

81

82

Chapman (cont)
    Malenda 11
    Serenah 28
    William T. 59
Chennault, Isaac 46
    Robert 60
Chesser, Cyrania J. 65
    James 65
    Wm. H. 59
Childress, Catherine 28, 35
    Susan 28
Chisholm, John 65
    Norton (Chism) 14
Choat, Esquire E. 39
    H. R. B. 27
    James 7
    Jane 28
    Nancy 3
    Prudy 7
    Sarah 12
    Thomas 26
Choate, John K. 60
Christian, Isham 24
    J. D. 38
    Jane 31
    Lotty 62
    Martha 24
    Martha J. 60
    Rhody 24
    Zilphy 25
Chronister, Arthur R. 52
    Elizabeth 32
    May 18
    Phillip 13
Churchwell, Ephrain 60
Clair, John G. 37
Clark, Jack 8
    Mary A. 41
    Susannah 60
    Wm. 20
Clay, Mary Ann 73
    Sarah Jane 54
Clayton, Elizabeth 68
    J. B. 63
    J. S. 69
    Martha 49
    Mary 61
    Rachel 37
    Richard 8, 37, 40
    Sarah Jane 42
    Stanford 37
    Susannah 56
    William 57
Clement, Chaney 53

Clemmons, Thomas 7
    William 40
Clendenin, Telia Ann 61
Clendennon, Theodore 74
Clifton, Candis 1
    Cyreney 22
    James 8
    Martha 54
    Mary 25, 32
    Sanny 8
Coalter, Nancy 28
Cobble, Isaac H. 73
Cochran, Eli 56
    Jane 66
    M. 38
    Malinda 40
    Rachel 70
    Robert 73
    William 44
Cockeral, Elizabeth 52
Cockerel, Jackson 45
Cockran, Eli 66
    William 63
Cockrell, Granville 72
Cody, Mary E. 66
Coffman, Elizabeth 62
    William H. 47
Cohorn, Olive 26
Coker, Huldy 21
    Jacob 43
    James T. 74
    Sally 20
Cole, Jane 60
    Rachael 24
    Washington L. 59
Coleburn, George W. 8
Colier, Adaline 56
    Elizabeth M. 53
Collins, Amanda L. 71
Comer, Aaron 40
    Elizabeth 62
    Martha 68
    Mary 1
    Rosannah 15
    Sarah 28
Conley, Catharine 8
Conly, M. 37
Conway, D. B. M. 67
Cook, Charles 36, 37
    Dyara 37
    James 8
    Joseph 39
    Louisa 38
    Mary J. 39, 69

Cook (cont)
  Peggy 1
  Sandel L. 42
  Stephen 38
  Susanah 38
  Susannah 37
  Thomas 19
  Vina 26
  William 21, 38
Cookburne, George W. 47
Cookrell, Lucretia J. 72
Cooper, Charity 11
  Cinthy 20
  Eli P. 66
  Ellen 10
  Robert T. 74
Copelin, Jacob 45
Corcoran, Patrick 72
Cosby, E. M. 40
Cossey, L. 38
Cothen, James 21
  Susan 21
Cotrell, Alpha 48
Cottrell, Martha 3, 68
  Nancy 7
Couch, Jan 42
  Joseph W. 50
Counce, William 31
Counts, John 37
  Marry 37
  William 3, 18
Courtney, Isaac 11
  Susanna 21
Cowen, Elizabeth 30
Cowers, Eliza P. 9
  John 36
Cowin, Lovenia E. 30
Cox, David 54
  Elisha 27
  Giles H. 65
  Isaac 54
  Mary Ann 56
  Moses 64
  Samuel 61
Crabb, Elizabeth Ann 74
  Foutain R. 45
  James H. 53
  Thomas W. 73
  Wm. P. 65
Craig, Adam 17
  Isabella 41
  Isaac N. 50
  James 47
  John N. 75

Craig (cont)
  Margaret A. 29
  Mary 17
  Mary D. 55
  Nancy 54
Creasy, Robert 58
Crews, Augustin 60
  Benjamin 60
  Benjamine 36
  Benjamon 38
  Elizabeth 63, 69
  James F. 50
  Jonas 47
  Jonathan 51, 57
  Joseph 56
  Kary A. 58
  Manerva 72
  Martha 56
  Mary A. 40
  Mary Ann 69
  Mary J. 70
  Nancy 37
  Sarah 39
  Sidney 53
  Susan 55
  Zachariah 52
Crisp, Elizabeth C. 18
  John 10
  Sarah 10
Crockett, David 6
Crofford, John 7
  William C. 47
Crook, Zerubbabel 55
Cross, Adaline 49
  C. W. 38
  James F. 62
  John 60
  Mary A. E. 45
  Thomas V. 72
  Vines H. 64
Crosthwait, Nancy 58
Crosthwaite, Joseph P. 6
Crostwait, Mary 58
Crow, Elizabeth 33
Culbirth, Mary Ann 62
Culbreth, Daniel 21
  Delia 21
Cunningham, Sara 3
  Solomon W. C. 28
  Thomas G. 70
  William F. 13
Curry, Elizabeth L. 59
  Green B. 48
  Jas N. 39

84

Curry (cont)
 Mary 59
 Thomas 66
 Thomas G. 65
Curtis, Adaline 61
 Elizabeth J. 69
 Isaac W. 59
 Martha M. 60
 Rachel 69
 Rebecca 7
 Thomas 61
Cutbirth, Ira 60
Dalton, David 36
 David B. 12
 Eliza 12
 Emeline 55
 John L. 41
 Jonathan 66
 Joseph M. 67
 Lewis 25
 Mary 59
 Susannah 7
 Toliver P. 31
Dame, Eliza 41
 James 74
 Mahala 48
 Malinda J. 41
 Margaret 50
 Martha 59
 Mary F. 69
 Nancy 42
Dancy, Carolina A. 43
Daniel, Caroline 65
 Harvey 41
Davidson, Joel 66
 John 41
 John D. 45
 Mary B. 53
 Sarah A. 64
 Sarah K. 32
Davis, Anna 58
 Any 26
 Branson 59
 Catharine 5, 72
 Daniel 42
 Dicey 54
 Elizabeth 33, 42
 Elizabeth Ann 58
 Emeline 41
 Franklin 64
 George A. 51
 Henry R. 17
 Isabella Jane 46
 James W. 4

Davis (cont)
 John 9, 46
 Levi 61
 Louisa 71
 Lucinda 42
 M. A. P. 44
 Maria 36
 Micajah 54
 Moses 72
 Nancy 34, 36
 Polly 12
 Rachel 4
 Rebecca 19, 20, 36
 Stephen L. 26
 William 7, 24, 53
 William C. 71
 Winney 10
Day, Elizabeth 2
 H. 23
 H. D. 37
 Henry 11
 Jane A. 10
 John B. 13
 July Ann 31
 Milley 3
 Nancy 15
Deason, Jane 6
Deavenport, M. W. 58
 Mary E. 52
 Nancy 51
Defoe, Thomas C. 69
Delk, George W. 66
Delozier, Ruhahar 46
Denton, Lemuel B. 1
Depriest, Jesse 40
 Regina 10
Derveast, Nancy 61
Devasure, Lady Jane 38
Diah, Andrew J. 55
Dial, Elizabeth 47
 James 57
 Joel 42
 Nancy 17
 Patrick 14
 Robert 6
 Rutha 38
 Winny 12
Dickey, G. M. 39
 Robert 70
Dickie, William M. 41
Dickson, John B. 44
 Lavonia A. 67
 Margaret 10
 Mary 13

Dickson (cont)
  Sam 26
  Spencer C. 61
  William 41
Dicus, Elijah 46
Dishough, Elizabeth J. 20
Dixon, Columbus F. 70
  Fountain J. 66
  James M. 67
Dobbin, A. T. 39
Dobbins, Eliz Ann 67
  Martha J. 65
Douglass, Jane E. 63
Down, Sady 3
Downes, Nancy J. 74
Downs, Parient 21
  Polly 10
Doyal, Martha 26
Doyl, Martha 35
Duckes, John L. 66
Duckworth, Eliz E. 69
  Sophia 24
Dueast, Jasper 66
  Susanah 40
Due-East, Mary E. 51
Duffield, Samuel L. 4
Dugger, Charles J. 39
Dunahoo, Alexander 14
Duncan, Angeline 11
  Cynthia E. 44
  D. L. 46
  David L. 19
  Eliza J. 3, 36
  Elizabeth 58
  John W. 44
  Mary A. 46
  Mary S. 22
  W. F. 62
  William S. 41
Dunlap, Elizabeth 28
  Matilda 16
Durbin, John G. 2
  Mary A. 54
  Sarah 38
  Susannah 41
Durly, Jno. J. 39
Earwood, Jesse 46
  Malinda 14
  Nancy 46
Eastes, William 14
Eaton, Catherine 41
  James 66
Eaves, Allen 59
  Jonathan 74

Eaves (cont)
  Jonathan M. 63
  John 56
  Rosannah 70
Eddins, Mary 3
Edleman, Aurey 22
  Elizabeth 30
Edmiston, Elihu 65
  Esther Elizabeth 1
  Margaret A. 33
  Mary P. 1
  Matilda 21
Edwards, Anny 1
  Jane 45
Elison, Andrew 17
Ellison, Franklin 58
  Samuel 23
Elton, Sarah M. 29
Emerson, John L. 53
English, Margaret 10
Ensson, (?) 37
Eose, Solon E. 45
Ervin, Sophiah 71
Escue, Samuel 49
Eskew, James 66
  Lety 60
Eskus, Unity 37
Essary, Mary Ann 59
  Ruth 63
Estes, Henry N. 62
  James D. 61
  Martha Ann 63
  Mary 72
  William 10
Ethridge, Mariah 48
  Rebecca 51
  Sally 9
  Sarah 60
  Thomas 38
  William 19
Evans, Amanda 46
  Cynthia 60
  Ezer 12
  Jane 58
  Josiah 60
  Sarah F. 44
Ezell, Edmond 33
  Edmund D. 6
  Lennuel A. 68
  Nancy Mary Ann 70
  Sarah Ann 6
  William 70
Fanning, James 56
Farmer, B. 14

Farmer (cont)
  Bracewell 26
  Elizabeth 31
  Mahaly 18
  Milly 28
  Sally 15
Farriss, Robert 45
Farrow, Nancy S. 38
Faught, Sarah 38, 40
Faust, Eleanor E. 66
Favour, Thomas 74
Fenney, Amanda 71
Ferrill, Eliz 60
  Ibby 72
Fields, Lewis G. 62
  Richard 52
Fifeny, (?) Nancy 12
Findley, Ealinor 9
Finley, Eleanor 65
  Mariah 55
Finney, Henry 71
  Sarah 58
Fisher, Amy 10
  Anderson M. 54
  Celia 56
  Elizabeth 14, 53
  Jeremiah J. 12
  John 20
  John P. 37
  Madison 56
  Nancy 65
  W. E. 38
Flake, Robert 12
Flakes, Lucy Ann T. 10
Flippo, George W. 56
  Nathaniel 60, 74
  Patrick 53
Floid, William C. 43
Flood, Lucy 30
  Lucy D. 23
Flournoy, Ann 18
  Elizabeth 12
Floyd, Analiza 60
  Jane 60
  John W. 71
  Jno. W. 39
  Mahala C. 62
  Marjoh E. 71
  William 65
Fogg, James M. 36
  William H. 63
Fondren, James 27
  John 21, 25, 35
  Sarah 19

Forest, Francis J. 18
Forgey, James 3
Fortenberry, Sarah 43
Foster, Angelina 36
  Angeline 12
  Catharine 69
  George W. 47
  Joel J. 67
  John F. 64
  Louise 12
  Manerva A. 68
  Manerva J. 67
  Margaret 29
  Mary Jane 54
  Reddick 45
  Simon P. 58
Foust, Aaron 67
  Christopher 11
  William 39
Frank, Francis M. 69
Franklin, (?) 29
  Elener 72
  Elias 71
  Martha 71
  Reuben 63
  Reubin 73
Franks, Caroline E. 21
  George W. 4, 28
  Martha E. 28
  Sarah E. 70
Frazier, Stephen S. 66, 73
Freeman, Edward R. 60
  Hannah 47
  Irvine T. 59
  Martha 45
French, Jacob 59
Fugat, Vina M. 72
Fuget, Mary 62
Fulks, Meredith 56
Fuller, Mary Jane 51
  William J. 53
Fullington, Ritta 50
Furguson, Maryann 38
Futrel, Leedy 11
Futrell, Ann 21
  Eliza Ann 58
Futril, W. H. 37
Gabel, Barnabas ("Barney")
  12
  Elias P. 58
  James E. 72
  John 56
  Thomas J. 49
Gaines, Elizabeth 28

Gaither, E. E. 57
  Isabella Jane 47
  John S. 52
  Matildy 6
Gallaher, Joseph G. 61
  Margret Ann 51
  Rebecca 66
Galloway, Josiah J. 68
  Nancy 10
Gambrell, Sally 11
Garden, T. 44
Garner, Arbina 48
  Cynthian 7
  Elisabeth 37
  John 11
  Lainer 34
  Lucinda 22
  Sarah 68
Garret, Nancy 21
Garrett, Manerva 54
  Michael 72
  Samuel 40
Gee, Robert 11
Gelespiee, Elisabeth 37
Gelison, John G. 72
Geton, Malinda 13
Gibbins, Laurey A. 69
Gibbons, James M. 58
  N. B. 46
Gibson, Isaac 15, 31
  Jas J. 37
  Malinda 23
  Roena 12
Gideon, Mary 14
  Rhoda 44
Gilbert, Elizabeth 57
  Elmira 26
  John 58
  Martha 42
  Wm. R. 32
Gilbreath, Mary 39
Gilespie, A. M. 63
  James H. 69
Gillespie, Newton M. 61
Gillispie, John A. 55
Gilmon, Margaret J. 63
Gilmore, Ann 41
  John S. 42
  Margaret J. 62
  Tennessee 59
Gist, Elizabeth 31
  James 41
  John 53
  Joshua 31

Gist (cont)
  Levi 37
  Margaret 4
  Nancy 16
Glass, William V. 39
Glover, Elizabeth 49
  Feliz 64
  Jesse B. 13
  Martha 56
  William 57
Goad, Lucy 71
  Sarah Jane 51
  William H. 71
Goats, Philip 37
Gobble, Isaac H. 73
Goble, Elias P. 37
  Elisha P. 36
Goff, Eliza J. 62
  Harriet Jane 47
  John C. 41
Goforth, Rachael 18
Goode, John 57
Gooden, Reuben 49
Goodman, Amos 52
Goodwin, Rebecca A. 67
Gordon, Arean 55
  Augustus B. 60
  Elizabeth 12
  Elvira M. C. 65
  Mary E. 50
  Nancy 66
  Nancy F. 49
  Sarah D. 71
  W. C. 44
  Zachariah E. 71
Gosnell, Benjamin 12
Gower, Catherine C. 52
  Charrity 7
  Eliza Ann 52
  John M. 66
  Manerva 65
  Nicholas 48
  Teressa C. 66
  William A. 53
  William F. 73
Gowers, John 37
Graham, John 37
Gray, (?) 13
  Elizabeth 2, 54
  Martha J. 66
  Robert 13
  Sarah 56
Green, Allen 42
  Ann 70

Green (cont)
  Anny 8
  Elizabeth 3, 43
  Ephraim B. 29
  Francis M. 67
  James M. 58, 61
  John 71
  Joshua 55
  Lewallen 36
  Marry 38
  Martha 52
  Martin 74
  Mary 42
  Miles M. 65
  Nace 48
  Octavia 14
  Priscilla 41
  Priscilla H. 51
  Sarah Ann 41
  Stephen 47
  Susan 66
  Vernettie 72
  Willia J. 42
  Winney A. 71
Greenhau, Edward B. 13
Greenhaus, John 39
Greenhaw, Emily 53
  Ephraim 51
  Sarah A. 68
Greenhow, Ephraim B. 36
Greenwood, Izeller 39
  William G. 35
Grenaway, Milley 5
Gresham, Catherine 30
  Ephraim 28
  George 12
  Nancy 33
  Solomon 23, 30
Griffin, Elizabeth 5, 28
  James 65
  Washington 66
Grigg, William 37
Griggs, Sarah Jane 69
Grimes, D. G. 36
  Jackson
  Mary 42
  Nancy 8
Grinway, Wm. 37
Grisham, Carolina 37
  Elizabeth 36
  James T. 64
  Mary 36
  William E. 49
Grisom, James M. 49

Grissam, John 42
Grissham, Rebecca A. 39
Grissom, Careline M. 67
  Catherine 59
  Dicy E. 41
  G. W. 38
  James 36
  John 40
  Laban 41
  Margaret A. 50
  Martha L. 67
  Mary S. 55
Guess, Jane 38
Guest, Catherine 12, 35
Guinn, Sarah 38
Gulley, Lewis 48
Gunter, Frances 51
Guthrie, Daniel 64
Gwinn, Eveline 58
  Louisa H. 75
  Mary 54
  Nancy 53
  Ruth L. 61
Gwyn, Mar 12
Gyst, Mary 13
Hackley, Shadrack 54
Hackney, Jackson H. 41
Hagan, A. W. 3
  Isaiah 60
  John 40
Hagens, A. W. 36
Haggins, Margaret 6
Hail, Dinah B. 46
  Evaline 37
  James E. 27
  Jane 16
  John A. 8, 36
  John W. 47
  Sally 27
  William F. 72
Hale, Charles D. 68
  Howard 52
  Isaac A. 52
  Sarah E. 58
Halford, B. 5, 9, 15, 23,
  31
  John R. 14
  Robt. E. 30
Hall, Camilla A. 67
  Sally 8
  Sarah Ann 38
  William 11
Halland, Harrison 66
Ham, Berry 44

Ham (cont)
David 72
Elizabeth 49, 72
John E. 45
Mary 55
Richard 57
William M. 50
Hambrick, Mary 23
Hamersley, Eliza 47
Hamilton, Herton 22
John 40
Sarah M. 52
William N. 41
Hamlet, Mary 40
Nancy 51
Hamm, Nancy 65
Hammonds, A. E. 44
E. J. 43
Mary C. 44
Mary J. 67
Melissa A. 70
Nancy C. 61
Willis 28
Hammons, Elizabeth 11
Henry 11
Morning 18
Hamsley, Robert 10
Hanks, G. W. 20
Hannah, Nancy 74
Hanner, Eliz J. 47
Harder, Margaret E. 55
Hardiman, Susan 67
Hardin, James H. 66
Jane J. 22
Nathan P. 40
Hare, Elizabeth 18
Harland, Julia 65
Sarah 73
Harlow, James 50
Sarah 27
Harmon, Hilliard 69
Harmons, John 57
Harrelson, Rachael 64
Rebeccah 31
William 31
Harris, Elizabeth 27
Harrison, America 27
Betsey 11
James B. 69
Sarah J. 45
William F. 50
Hartless, Eliz A. 58
Hartsfield, Celia Ann 54
Mathew 43

Hartwell, Elizabeth 10
Hartwick, Aso O. 35
Coonrood 5
Easter 38
Elizabeth 6
George 26
Mathew 40
William 13, 36
Harvell, Alexander 52
Harvey, Richard 49
Harwell, Samuel 32
Hatcher, John E. 68
Haynes, J. P. 37
Kiziah E. 50
M. E. 44
Hays, John 38
Head, Francis D. 71
Heffington, A. M. 42
Anna H. 64
Daniel 37
Emeline 63
Rachael 59
Sally 37
Hefly, Mary 39
Mary E. 42
Heldridge, Nancy 17
Helton, Abraham 46
Adaline 71
Sally 26
Hemphill, Nancy 17
Hencely, Barbary 17
Henderson, James F. 47
Polly 31
Hendrix, Almira Jane 49
Mary 22
Nancy D. 66
Sarah 61
Simon 49
Henry, Elizabeth 5
John 59
William 22
Hensley, Benjame 36
James 29
Lucinda 20
Mary V. 47
William H. 48
William N. 68
Hensly, Nancyann 37
Henson, Wesley D. 71
Heralson, Diannah 7
Elizabeth 7
Robert 7
Heralston, E. 5
Herbert, Calvin L. 57

Herralston, Lavina 19
Herrin, Ageline 14
  C. J. 14, 16
  Charles 21
Herring, Polly 33
Hetamer, Polly 32
Hiatt, Lorra 56
Hickman, Wm. 62
Hicks, Anny 12
  Carolina 56
  James P. 12
  John 13
  Mary 71
  Susan 13
Hide, Elizabeth 25
Higdon, Rebecca 45
Higgins, Jerry 43
Higgs, Jane 52
  Jesse 36, 37, 58
  Mary A. 53
High, A. V. B. 68
Hight, Benety Ann 23
Hightower, Nancy 24
Hill, Berry 30
  Catharine 68
  Eliza 44
  Lewis 29
  Louisa 52
  Lucinda 26, 34
  Margaret 48
  R. J. 25
  Sarah Ann 29
  Sarah C. 53
  Spicy 2
Hillhouse, Elvira M. 71
  Geo. D. 39
  John S. 2
  Wilson 26
Hindsley, May 29
Hinsley, Charlotte 10
Hinson, Jackson 49
Hodge, Hubbard 50
  Robert 52
  Telitha 60
Hodges, John W. 74
Hoge, Sally 12
Hogg, Oma 4
  Robert 24
  Tebitha P. 24
Hoke, Wiley 52
Holden, Cynthia 63
  Thomas 52
Holland, Amos Prater 62
  Andrew J. 55

Holland (cont)
  Chaney 59
  Jane M. 21
  Leletha Ann 49
  Martha A. 39
  Matilda 27
  Polly 5
  Thomas 30
  Thomas D. 59
Hollis, Eli W. 57
  Ibby 66
  Jasper N. 73
  Sinah 12
Holloway, Catharine 41
  Elizabeth 47
  John 15
  Pleasant 47
  Sally 20
  Sarah 4, 35
Holly, Mary 43
Holt, Elizabeth 50
  Manerva Jane 54
  William R. 15
Holtsford, Juliann 71
Hood, Cathrine 33
Hooper, Ann E. 61
  Harriet M. G. 53
  James 67
  Mary 64
Horn, Anderson 74
  Angeline 47
  Elizabeth 65
  Nancy 13
  Thomas 15
Horne, Edward B. 60
  William P. 51
Horton, Nancy Ann 16
Howard, Mary 49
  Polly 27
  Sam 39
  Samuel 48
  Sarah 21
  William 47
Howell, Johnathan 72
Hudson, C. C. 63
Huggins, James 70
  Mary E. 71
Hughes, David 69
  Higah 46
  James E. 64
  James F. 56
  Jeptha 67
  Joseph 48
  Nancy L. 57

91

Hughes (cont)
  S. J. 34
Hughs, Jesse 71
  Levinch 44
  Sarah 46
  William 4
Humphries, Elizabeth 3
Hunt, Catharine 41
  Elizabeth 55
  Eveline E. 45
  Fountain D. 45
  George O. 48
  Jane 33
  Nancy 42
  Nancy C. 40, 57
  William M. 56
Hunter, Mary A. 8
Hurst, Jemime V. 40
Hutcheson, Alfred 57
  Elizabeth 27
  Jesse 20
  John M. 72
  Mary 5
  Sarah 5
Hutchison, Sarah 35
Ingram, Angeline 66
  Elihu 56
  Mary E. 73
  Nancy 44
  Susan 18
  William 41
Inman, Joseph C. 73
  Louisa J. 64
  Meshack 32
  Sally 19
  Zachus 7
Inmon, Joseph C. 44
  Margarett M. 72
Innman, John C. 47
Insor, Wm. 36
Irby, Eliza S. 1
  Henry 35
Irvine, Anonymous 2
Isaacs, Elizabeth 2
Iseley, William 58
Ivey, Eliz. L. 64
  Louisa 66
  Margaret 61
  William L. 65
Izely, Delila 57
Jackson, Beckey 17
  David C. 10
  Eliza A. 56
  Hannah 68

Jackson (cont)
  John 49
  Matthew 56
James, Andrew J. 35
  Betsey 2
  Manerva 66
Jane, Tahny 31
Jeffries, John W. 62
Jeno, Polly 9
Johns, Enoch G. 49
  Lydia 14
  Mahala 6
  Matilda 53
Johnson, Abner 70
  Elizabeth 62
  Leaner 21
  Lucreska 25
  Mary Ann 50
  Mary Jane 70
  Robert 21, 23
  Susan 60
Johnston, D. C. 40
  E. A. 37
  Elizabeth 16, 40
  Elizabeth H. 22
  Inda 12
  James M. 55
  John A. 16
  Martha 52
  Mary 30, 31, 35, 49
  Nancy M. 62
  Rebecca 3
  Saml 45
  Sarah 8
  Sarah Jane 52
  Thomas T. 45
  William R. 33
Jones, And. J. 38
  Calvin 64
  Elendor 49
  Elias 52, 73
  Jacob S. 59
  James 42, 60
  Josiah 65
  Milly 15
  Phillip 33
  Phoebe 33
  Sally 40
  Sarah 71
  Sarah E. 68
  Stephen 36, 37
  Susan 13
  William A. 42
  Winey 37

Joyce, Ferdinan F. 68
  William 49
Judge, John 57, 70
Kanaday, Telitha 14
Keelin, Elizabeth A. 57
Keenan, Nancy B. 40
Keese, Elijah W. 22
Keith, Haywood 46
  Nathan 38
Kelley, Margret Jane 43
  Parnecy 43
Kelly, Daniel L. 72
  Elizabeth 42
  George 45
  Hannah 49
  James 16, 30
  Malinda 42
  Margaret 49
  Martha 55
  Mary 47
  Mary Ann 54
  R. L. 37
  Robert 13
  Robert J. 48
  Susan 63
  Thomas E. 58
  Thomas M. 68
  William J. 66
  Wm. 48
Kelsey, Sarah 73
Kelso, James R. 48
Kelsy, Mary 65
Keltner, Annul 20
  Nancy L. 51
Kelton, Martha J. 73
  William D. 46
Kenneddy, Mary C. 45
Kennedy, Nancy 62
  S. R. 62
  Sarah A. 72
  Weakley G. 69
  Wm. H. 64
Kennemer, Edmond H. 58
Kellel, Emanuel J. 38
Kidd, James B. 46
  John A. 49
  Josiah W. 40
  Martha H. E. 74
Kilbarn, Catharine 40
Kilbern, Carroll 37
Kilborn, Joel 41
Kilburn, David 55
  Elizabeth 21, 46, 52
  Fanny 48

Kilburn (cont)
  Frances 49
  Hannah 57
  James 44
  John M. 58
  Martha 9
  Mary 9, 50
  Nancy L. 48
  Sarah 15
  William 63
Kimball, G. W. 38
Kimbrel, George W. 55
Kinbrell, King 69
Kindrick, Susan 59
King, Elizabeth A. E. 56
  James H. 74
  Mary 37
Kinnaman, John 56
Kirk, Cinthy 16
  Elizabeth 57
  Emily J. 56
  Lewis M. 56, 70
  Lucy 70
  Martha 45
  Mary F. E. 47
  Robert 57
  Wm. F. 56
Kirksey, Jesse B. 54
  Mary H. 66
Klyce, Ruth Ann 68
Kosure, J. B. 10
  L. B. 36
Kyle, John 59
Lacroix, John J. 67
Lad, Martha 74
Laffoon, E. A. 41
Lakey, Polly 14
Lamay, Nathan 73
Lancaster, Brad 20
  Braddock 36
  Eleanor 57
  Malinda 47
  Nancy 53
  Sarah 42
Lane, Lucindy 8
Lanier, Mel. 18
  Turner 35
Lathem, Andrew M. 68
Lauderdale, Elijah 63
Lawhon, Thomas H. 54
Lawrence, James H. 73
Lay, Adaline 68
  G. S. 37
  Nancy 41

Lynan, Lucy M. 54
Lyons, Malinda 51
  Permelia 9
  Pernia 2
  Plate 26
Lysle, Elvira 4
Mack, Joannah 27
Madden, Joshua L. 59
Maimon, Malissa 50
Majors, Sirena C. 30
Mallard, Amitha 60
Maner, Lucinday 36
Manford, E. W. 61
Manuel, Fenny 30
  Lurany 2
  Payton 44
  Philip 55
Marcum, Mary 51
  Nancy 66
  Samuel 46
  William 1
  Wm. 44
Markham, Charlotte 20
  Eliza 36
  Julian 4
  Lewis 26
  Jonathan 40
Marks, John H. 62
Martin, Elizabeth 51
  James 64
  John B. 49
  Martha C. 59
  Marry 44
  Samuel H. 37
  Sarah 20
  Sarah A. 72
  William 73
  William H. 55
  Wm. C. 54
Maryman, James 10
  Telithy 10
Mason, Eliza 15, 36
  John 24
  Mary A. R. 61
  Nathaniel 6, 12
  Samuel 29
  Samuel E. 42
  Sarah 37
  Warren 38
  Warrer 18
Massey, J. D. 71
  Nancy 61
  Pleasant 54
  Richard 18
  Sarah J. 66

Matthews, Eliz 38
  Elizabeth 58
  G. T. 36
  Jacob 5
  Jane 32
  John 31
  Mary J. 65
  Mary M. 39
  Mary T. 70
  Sally 31
  Stephan 23
  Stephen 7, 23
  Stephen J. 33
  Thomas J. 16
  Thos. J. 17, 19, 23
  Vilothy 18
  W. W. 2
Mauldes, Susanna P. 32
Mauldin, Benjamin F. 53
  Nancy R. 38
Maxey, Elizabeth 32
  James B. 66
  Thomas H. 70
May, Anna 25
  Daniel W. 40, 72
  Elizabeth Ann 73
  Emeline 39
  James 6
  John C. 42
  Mary 38
  Mary Ann 35
  William C. 43
Mayhew, Emeline 47
Mayhu, Mahala 38
Mayhue, Alford 37
  Palina 37
  Pauline 36
McAlester, Elvina J. 73
McAnally, Anna 11
  Eli 9
  Elizabeth 4
  Elmira 68
  John 41
  Lucinda 63
  Manerva 10
  Mary A. 44
  Milton 56
  N. C. 63
  Winston 40
McAnnally, Francis J. 50
  Lois D. 44
  Mariah 50
McBride, A. R. 74
  J. L. 37
  James D. 48

McBride (cont)
  Nancy 42
  Thomas M. 68
McCabe, W. P. A. 20
McCafferty, Arilla 6
  W. G. 70
McCain, Hugh 21
McCalister, Mary Ann 42
  Salina 31, 36
McCallister, Mary Ann 18
McCann, Hannah 26
  John 29
  Moses 42
McCareby, Zilphy 4
McCarstin, John 61
McCaskill, Mehala C. 67
  Wm. J. A. 67
McCewen, Lucinda 56
  Marinda 54
McClain, Ephram 61
  John Jr. 10
McClamock, David L. 74
McClannahan, James 74
McClendon, Manerva J. 69
  Nathan 20
McClure, Mary Ann 69
McCracken, Louisa 21
  Mary 38
McCrackin, Calvin 19
  John J. 37
  Nancy E. 63
  Roxana W. 63
McCrory, Mary A. 74
  Thomas 63
  Thomas J. 48
McCutchen, William 69
McDanell, James 72
McDonald, John G. 6, 11,
  16, 27
  Levi 6
  Nancy 6
  Thos. A. 69
McDougal, An Jane 10
  Catharine 4
  Daniel 59
  Eleanor 37
  Eleanor J. 59
  Eliza 50
  Margaret 12
McElyeo, Mary 24
  Samuel 24
McEwin, Moniah 39
McFall, James 18
McFalls, Ollivia 7

McGee, Caloway 52
  Daniel K. 70
  Elizabeth 44
  John 61
  Leroy 49
  Mary J. 64
  Micajah 39
  Susannah 53
  William R. 52
McGree, Henry 51
  Lucinda V. O. J. 57
McGwire, Sally 49
McHughs, Martha 38
McIntire, Catharine 19
  Nancy 28
McIntyre, Amy 6
  Daniel W. 26
  Hugh C. 4
  James 2
  Jas. 37
  Joe 21
MckAnally, Wilson D. 44
McKaskil, Mary Jane 62
McKeu, Jane 14
McKew, Charles 26
  Sally 26
McKinney, M. F. 39
McKmillon, Susan 43
McKnight, Hugh 39
  Mary E. 68
  Nancy A. 43
  William, Jr. 1, 22
McLaren, Charles R. 57
  Elizabeth 3
  James 35
  Mary J. E. 55
  Mary Jane 51
  R. C. 10
  Robert L. 58
  Sarah E. 50
  Sarah J. 70
  Susan 63
McLean, Charles L. 46
  M. R. 36
  Melchesedick 51
  Nancy 11, 35
  R. I. 29
  Sarah A. 63
  Sarah Jane 65
  Samuel 63
McLearen, Charles K. 42
McLemore, Barbary 24
McLusky, Isaac 39
McMackin, Adelia 54

McMackin (cont)
Elizabeth A. 70
John 52
Rosilla W. 8
Stephen A. 71
McMasters, Daniel 35
Elizabeth 32, 57
Hannah 40, 59
John 57, 68
Jonathan 64
Leander 65
Mary 47
Nancy 58
Rachel E. 48
Sarah 17
Zilpha 39
McMillan, Elizabeth L. 69
McMillin, James 6
Nelson 17
McMillon, Alexander W. 61
McNeill, Catharine B. 45
Effa 62
John P. 69
L. 41
Nancy C. 65
McQuigg, A. T. 7
Sarah 7
Ticey 67
McRory, Thomas 2
McWhirter, John F. 22
Malinda 31
Mary G. 22
Sarah R. 64
William C. 62
Meadows, Eupphene 67
George W. 55
Wm. S. 48
Meek, Giles M. 57
Melton, Delila 57
Elijah 5, 19, 55
Franky 25
Riley M. 51
William 20
Meredith, A. B. 53
Merit, Silas 36
Merrit, Silas 37
Mewborn, Asa D. 48
Lucinda 48
Miatt, Eliz. 46
Michie, George 23
Wm. 30
Micke, Mises 3
Miles, Elizabeth 54
Hosea 65

Miles (cont)
James 41
Lucinda 74
Martha 60
Solomon 18
William 63
Willis F. 63
Miller, Alexander 47
Charlott 39
Eliza 65
Elizabeth 2
John 24, 73
John P. 43
Joseph 34
Lucretia 42
Manerva J. 68
Mary 27
Minerva Jane 15
Purgy 15
Millin, Darkis 16
Mills, Nathaniel 67
Millstead, William 24
Milton, Philip 43
Mires, Catherine 53
Emily 69
Mitchell, Araminta 42
Cinthy 32
Elijah 33
G. B. 44
Sarah Ann 45
Thomas 42, 68
William 57
Winney C. 72
Wm. R. 51
Mobley, Alsey 72
Edward 32
John R. 57
P. A. 47
William J. 45
Molton, Sarah 40
Monday, Julia 48
Lourinda 37
Lucinda 36
Montgomery, D. J. 38
James C. 39
Mailida 12
Nancy C. 50
Wm. 37
Moody, Catharine 27
Darcus 25
Dorcus 25
Elizabeth 57
Jane 66
M. H. 39

Moody (cont)
Martin H. 60
Mary Ann 39
Moarning (Reed) 3
Moses 62
Polly 27
Sabra 20
Thomas J. 55
William 20
Wm. D. 70
Moore, Ann 34
Benjamin W. 54
David L. 22
Dicey 26
George 53
John M. 67
Martha A. 51
Milly 39
Sally 15
Samuel 30
Stephen 41
Wm. J. W. 24
Moores, Wm. C. 47
Morison, Berry 59
Morow, Nathaniel 33
Morris, Benjamin 63
Carroll 17
Elijah, 60
Elizabeth Ann 22
Elizabeth M. 35
Felix G. 54
George W. 53
Hiram 57
Isaac 36
Jackson J. 46
John W. 50
Laydia W. 15
Martha E. 46
Mary Jane 57
Mary L. 66
Nancy E. 60
Rebecca M. 50
Sameul C. 64
Shadrack 17
William 20, 51
Morrison, Elizabeth A. 74
James C. 68
Joseph A. 71
Nancy 59
Morrow, Archibald 28
Frances 51
John 69
Mariah 51
Mary 24

Morrow (cont)
Rebecca 22
Sara F. 51
Stephen 65
Wm. F. 64
Wm. S. 67
Morton, Hannah A. 27
Moss, Janilly A. 55
Thomas W. 54
Moten, Charles 59
Moton, Isaac 38
Murphy, Archibald 34
Carolina H. 24
E. B. 44
Edward 55
Eliza Jane 73
George 48
William 57
Murrah, Saml. F. 64
Murrell, Jeffrey 70
Myers, Arena 46
Cassey Ann K. 46
Charles H. 50
Deanah 69
Nancy 56
Perry 43
Nail, Archer 28
Napier, Eliza Ann 14
G. F. 16
Neale, Mary Jane 63
William T. 68
Neely, Sarah 57
Nelson, Hugh 42
James 66
Jane 50
John 19
Polly 19
Robert 17
Runey 33
Sarah 19
Nevill, James A. 68
Newburn, Eli 36
Newgent, Mary E. 72
Newton, Eliza 33
James H. 52
Jeptha 44
Katharine 70
M. D. 10
Martha A. 58
Mary Ann 33
Robert 54
Sarah Ann 52
Ursley 45
W. C. 38

Newton (cont)
  William E. 22
  Wm. E. 70
Nichols, Eliza J. 70
  James C. 24
  Jóhn A. 66
Nickson, Elizabeth 2
Nipper, Eleanor 21
  James 69
Nixon, George H. 3
Noblitt, Elizabeth 27
Norman, Frances M. 64
  Hannah C. 64
  Lewis 35
  Mary A. 69
  Nancy 63
  S. L. 40
  Wm. M. 65
  Wm. P. 13
Normines, Amy 22
North, Ira 63
Norwood, James S. 61
  Mary J. 67
  Nancy 56
  Sarah Ann 69
Nowlin, G. W. H. 69
  Lucy J. 69
  Phillip T. B. 74
Null, Alsey 11
  Christeny 32
  Jane 5
  Milley 34
  Nancy 2, 29
  Phillip 32
  Polly 13
  Susan 14
Nutt, Rachael E. 73
O'Bryant G. W. 74
Oakley, Jesse 59
Odam, Cely 29
Odom, Dempsey 8
  John 31
  Malissa 44
  Scily 5
Oldham, Nancy 15
Olive, Griscilda 67
Oliver, Francis M. 69
Ons, Harrison 67
  Nancy 67
Orr, Margaret J. 61
Osborn, A. G. 38
  B. F. 46
  Mary C. 53
Osburn, A. G. 56

Osburn (cont)
  Charlotte 58
  Eliza 49
  Elizabeth 64
  Juliann 59
  Margaret 58
  Martha Jane 45
  Noble 47
  Polly 29
  Samuel 52
  William 49
Overstreet, Berry C. 45
Owens, Ridden B. 60
  Zachariah 66
Pace, Jackson 63
  Thomas 27
  William R. 61
Pain, Daniel 40
Paine, Joseph L. 18
  Susan 33
Palmer, Martha 73
Palmore, Claborn 68
Parker, Artimissa R. 58
  Elizabeth 52
  Jalina 52
  James 11
  John 64
  Mary A. 9
  William L. 56
Parkes, Frances 57
  M. J. 54
Parks, Elvira D. 21
  Lovick P. 43
  Tilman B. 26, 34
Parrett, Margaret 26
Parter, James G. 40
Pate, Thomas 30
Patterson, Daniel 72
  Eliza 58
  Flora 6
  Martha 62
  Thomas 8
Patteson, B. M. 70
Payne, Harden 24
Pearce, Ann 22
  Caroline 23
  Daniel 22
  Everett A. 39
  George W. 42
  Harriet 4
  James 68
  John R. 53
  Marcum 2
  Raford F. 62

Pearce (cont)
  Roford F. 47
  Unita Ann 24
  Winneford 49
Peare, R. F. 71
Pelt, Elizabeth 65
Pennington, Abraham 68
  Barbary J. 59
  Candace 52
  Cyrena 5
  D. N. 74
  David 17, 56
  Eliz M. 61
  Eliza J. 70
  Elizabeth 14, 39
  Isaac 59
  Isaac W. 41
  J. D. 38
  Jacob 61
  Jacob M. 51
  Jacob W. 48
  John W. 49, 55
  Joseph M. 45
  Leroy 23
  Martha E. 74
  Nancy A. 70
  Phillip M. 51
  Rhoda 56
  Sarah 48
  Thomas J. 73
  Tomsey 55
  Wm. J. 69
Penny, James 66
Peoples, Elizabeth 15
Peoteet, Lucinda 23
Percy, Eliza 66
Perkins, A. M. 1, 30
Pernell, Harriet 62, 63
  Sarah M. 63
Perremore, Sary 6
Perrimon, Martha 20
Perry, John 37
Perrymore, Adaline 50
  Arritta 46
  Mary Ann 48
Petty, David 51
  Martha 7, 35
  Martha E. 62
  Nancy 36
  Rebecca 47
Pharr, Nancy P. 74
Philips, James 45
  Rachel 38
Phillips, Am. B. 10

Phillips (cont)
  Rebecca 13
Pickard, Alex C. 40
  Amanda 45
  Barbary J. 57
  Elizabeth 25
  Henry S. 61, 70
  John J. 61
  Lucy 68
  Martha A. 53
  Sally 3
  Sarah C. 38
  Synthia H. 56
Pierce, Elizabeth 57
  George W. 57
Pillow, Levi 63
  Stephen D. 72
  Wm. A. 67
Pippins, Martha J. 42
  Pricilla 8
Polk, Richard 43, 63
Pollock, Alexander 71
  Elisha C. 71
  Elisha K. 45
  Eliza A. 68
  Eveline J. 50
  Frances 38
  Henrietta C. 54
  John W. 50
  Mahala J. 60
  Marry 37
  Martha Ann 73
  Mary 39
  Mary (Polly) 11
  Reda 41
  Sarah C. 60
  Susanah 36, 37
  William 24
Ponds, Eliza J. 52
  Mary Ann 53
  Sabra P. 55
Pool, Parthena A. 42
Pope, Addison 40
  Drucillah 74
  Edith 66
  John W. 44
  Martha 13
  Rebecca 43
Poplin, Mary 46
Poppe, Rachal 44
Porter, Emily F. 64
  John N. 54
  Mariah 63
  Thomas L. 12

Porter (cont)
William 31
Poteet, Eliza 64
Henry N. 58
James 53
Jno. P. 39
Levi R. 3
Rebecca 15
Sady 3
Sally 15
Samuel 3
Samuel D. 24, 27
Susannah 56
Poteete, Jackson, 56
Potete, George 68
Potts, Elizabeth 63
Jesse 48
Powel, Catharine 48
James 39
Lucretia 28
Phebe 39
Powell, A. J. 74
Benj. D. 65
Calvin A. 67
Jane 57
Lucinda 22
Sary 10
Prewitt, Henry 41
Price, Elizabeth 3
John 23, 24
Patsy 23
Sarah 16
Winny 11
Prier, Martha 72
Sarah 50
William 53
Prince, Labern 73
Tabitha 62
Prior, Dicy 44
Martha 66
Nathan C. 44
Pryer, D. B. B. 69
Elizabeth H. 24
Frances 4
Hannah A. 71
Jonathan T. 37
Pullen, Ann E. 65
Eliza J. 52
James 45
Manerva Ann 49
Martha E. 74
Mary 39
Sarah L. 39
Pullin, Milley 5

Pursell, Elendor 51
Putman, Samuel 69
Quillan, Wm. N. 67
Quillen, Charles 69
Elvina 56
William 11, 20
Quillin, Parmelia 60
Rackley, Aggy 2
Elizabeth 2
Lucinda 54
Martha 10
Pattsey 19
Pasons 25
William 40
Wm. 24
Rackly, Elizabeth 35
Radford, Mary 17
Rainey, Isaac 22
Mary B. 41
Ramsey, John 24
Rebecca E. 70
Rufus G. 56
Ramsy, James J. 43
Randals, Nancy 65
Randolph, James 72
Ranolds, Sarah 17
Ratliff, Angeline 51
Barbary 39
David 31
Malinda 48
Nancy 67
Obed 59
William 51
Ray, Alexander 58
Ann 32
Elizabeth C. 57
Elizabeth Frances 74
George 63
Jane 43, 53
Letty 2
Mahala J. 73
Margaret 33
Milly 55
Selina 39
Thomas 62
Rea, Elizabeth 48
John B. 73
Mary S. 67
Nancy E. 70
Polly 2
Read, Eliza A. 72
Reddell, Catharine 57
Henry 38
J. L. 74

Reddell (cont)
James M. 57
John L. 62
Joseph 58
Nancy 41
Permelia 59
Robert A. 60
Redden, Nancy 69
Reddy, Lewis 30
Redin, Martha 40
Reed, Elizabeth 8
Rebecca 28
Reeder, David D. 56
Reese, John A. 18
Reeves, William 54
Renfro, Jesse 67
Retch, Daniel A. 62
Revell, Elizabeth 64
Reynolds, Sally 25
William 25
Rhea, Mary A. 41
Rhods, James F. 71
Richards, E. M. M. 50
Huldah 33
Mahala 48
Richardson, A. O 62
A. W. 72
Allen 44
Ann J. 42
E. 43
E. J. 36
Eliz. Ann 63
Eliza Ann 33
Elizabeth J. 6
Emeline 40
Francis 73
Franklin 55
John C. 35
L. E. 43
Lucretia 37
Mark 39
Mary 49
Nancy 56
Sarah M. 71
Thomas A. 35
Wm. 48
Richey, Ann M. 72
Emily E. 72
Richie, Susa 7
Richison, Rachel 30
Rickard, William P. 70
Rickets, Wm. S. 68
Rickman, John H. 69
Judge C. 49

Rickman (cont)
Levicia 58
Riddell, Mary Eleanor 42
Samuel J. 71
Sarah M. 49
Riddle, Amanthus M. 48
Cynthia A. 47
Delila 53
James A. 48
James M. 37
John 46
John H. 47
Lucinda 46
Nancy M. 40
Rosannah 45
William C. 47
Rider, Jefferson B. 67
Rosannah 59
Riggin, Dice 48
Riggs, Albert W. 50
John H. 46
Right, Lovice 19
Shu Hursaid 27
Right, William W. 44
Rinck, Margaret A. 61
Roach, Julia A. 61
Mary Eliz 52
Matthews 43
Nancy Jane 73
Roaland, Polly 21
Roberts, A. F. 44
Martha 48
Nicy 40
Real J. 9
Rial J. 5, 26, 30
Thomas 35
Thomas J. 44
Thos. J. 35
Roberson, Barbary 15
Elizabeth E. 4
Robertson, (?) 20
Cinthy 29
James 48
John 51
Mary 15
Milly 37
Thomas 26
Thos. J. 65
Rochards, Frances 9
Rochell, Rufus 53
Rockley, Josiah W. 36
Mary 63
Rodes, Faithy 21
Rodgers, Catharine 43

Rodgers (cont)
Sally 5
Rogers, B. H. 30
C. K. 64
Clarasey 19
James F. 62
Joseph E. 53
M. B. 71
Matilda 59
Rebecca 11, 59
Theodore 58
Roland, Elanor C. 16
Wm. C. 66
Rollantree, C. 37
Roper, Elizabeth 69
Milley Jane 68
Rose, Francis M. 67
James M. 43
William M. 62
Rosebum, John 44
Ross, James M. 27
Rosser, Martha 65
Rosson, Elizabeth 9
Mary 39
Rebecca Ann 52
Sally 33
Roundtree, Y. P. 37
Rowland, Sally 12
Runnels, A. 45
Russ, Matthew G. 67
Rutledge, Sally 23
Sailoers, Daniel 33
Sailors, Daniel 57
John 47
Sara 61
Samford, Louisa A. 71
M. M. 59
Robt. N. 46
Sanders, Calvin 48
Elizabeth J. 74
G. W. 40
George 17
Himbrick 36
Jacob 42
Jesse 26
Jesse F. 48
Joseph 20, 25, 27
Rehico 44
Sandy, Nancy 57
Sanford, James G. 39
L. M. 53
William K. 32
Sapplington, John 19
Saterfield, David 39

Saunders, Aaron 2
Saylors, Mary 46
Nicholas 53
Scaggs, Thomas G. 65
Scales, Peter 59
Spicy 22
Schoals, Miss 44
Scholes, Mariah 58
Scott, Anne 60
Berry 57
Eliza Jane 72
Elizabeth 57
Samuel S. 41
Seaton, Lewis 54
Security, William Moody 15
Sellers, John 39
Senter, Peggy 19
Sessums, Dianah V. 32
Julena 31
Leucinda C. 26
Martha 4
Setters, Martha E. 63
Shackelford, Hetty 22
Marthy 8
Mary A. N. (Nancy) 22
Maryan 43
Nettie 36
Thomas J. 73
Shannon, A. G. 45
Eliza J. 58
Sharber, Thomas W. 57
Sharp, Anny 1
Basil 8
Elizabeth 10
George F. 25
H. R. 45
Henry 1, 19
Jane 23
Mary A. 36
Pearcy 21
Starkey 21
Shaw, Mary H. 71
Nancy 54
Shay, Geo. 41
Shelton, Amy 10
Greenberry 48
George W. 62
Hezekiah 15
Lear 15
Wesley 32
Sheppard, James H. 66
Mary Jane 45
Shields, John 55
Shimpman, W. J. 36

Shipman, Jane 50
Shirley, John 28
Shook, Riley 56
　Sarah Jane 73
Short, Emeline 47
　James A. 70
　James M. 46
Simmons, Wada 31
　Wm. H. 54
Simms, James E. 55
　Martha 35
　Nancy 64
Simonton, Adelaide 5
　Angeline A. 61
　G. F. 21
　Jane 4
　Sarah 9
　William 41
Simpson, Elizabeth 20
　Evelina 9
　Isabella 40, 52
　Mary A. 63
　Nancy 35
　Samuel C. 71
　William 58
Sims, Elizabeth 42
　Jesse 5
Singleton, Letiha 35
　Letitha 5
Skillern, L. V. 37
　Martha 63
　Rebecca 53
　Susan G. 49
Smith, A. B. 71
　Abrin 50
　Adaline 54
　Alfred 52
　B. A. 56
　Caroline M. 40
　Chapley 61
　Clark 21
　Delila 59
　Elijah 70
　Elisibeth 38
　Elizabeth 60
　Eliza 18, 37
　Eliza J. 67
　George W. 28
　Henry S. 67
　James 8
　Jane 69
　Jasper 46
　John W. 35
　L. C. 74

Smith (cont)
　Lewis H. 43
　Louisa Jane 54
　Louisa W. 67
　Lucinda 46
　Margaret M. 66
　Mariah 54
　Martha J. 70
　Martin H. 74
　Mary 32, 35, 66
　Myranda 70
　Patsey 6
　Rachael E. 52
　Sara Ann 50
　Susan C. 54
　Synthia 25
　Thomas B. 69
Snodgrass, Barsheba 35
　Barshena 22
　Elizabeth 1
　L. D. 41
　Margaret 24
　Martha 40
Snow, Franklin 52
　Washington 49
Spain, Caroline 54
　Levina 59
Span, Reuben L. 57
Spears, Barnett 51
　Calvin 70
　Dickson 55
　Elizabeth 55
　Elizabeth A. 44
　Evaline 71
　Hasten 27, 28, 71
　J. K. 70
　John R. 38
　Joseph 46
　Libey 26
　Mary 51
　Nicholas 51, 69
　Richard 46
　Sally 17
　Sarah 11, 63
　Sibbey 20
　William R. 52
Speer, Aaron C. 72
　America H. 72
Spencer, Ambrose 3
　Eleanor 37
　Elizabeth P. 72
　Isaac N. 73
　Jane 56
　Moses 8

Taylor (cont)
  Mis G. 43
  Soloma G. M. 71
  Susan 55
  Susannah R. 16
  William 43
Tays, Cyntha 21
  Gney 8
  Sarah F. 55
Teas, James 31
Templeton, Louisa 17, 35
Tenneson, James S. 59
Tennesson, Jno. B. 64
Tennisson, Benjamin 30
Tennyson, Betsey 27
Terrell, Susannah 25
Terry, Nicholas 65, 69
Tesseson, W. M. 70
Tharp, William S. 73
Thomas, Joseph 23
  Temperance 6
Thompkins, M. M. 44
Thompson, Ebenezer 2
  Elisa 39
  Elizabeth 74
  Hilliard J. 42
  James W. 65
  Lurainey 14
  Margaret 48
  Margaret Ann 59
  Sarah F. 43
  Wm. P. 60
Thornton, Marinda 20
  Sara 66
  Sparting 35
  Thomas N. 12
  Wm. W. 51
Tice, Joseph 46
Tidwell, Carling M. 63
  Isaac 41
  Maryann 38
  Silas 48
Tinnon, Rosalinds 47
Tipper, Silas 56
Tipton, A. L. 62
Todd, Julia F. 40
  Malinda C. 28
  William J. 60
Tole, George W. 46
Tomblin, Moses 3
Tomlinson, Louisa 52
Tooten, Ann 38
  Dicy 72
  Sarah 46

Toys, Cyntha 36
  Jas. C. 44
Tracet, Rebecah 20
Tracy, Amy 26
  Eliza Ann 48
  Levinah 30
  Martha 30
  Sarah 21
  Tannehill 30
  Tanneyhill 52
Trip, Elizabeth 24
  Rebecca 30
Tripp, Cynthia 56, 65
  Harlow A. 47
  Mary 60
  Wady 48
  William 73
Trobough, Julia 73
Trorbaugh, Catherine 47
  Daniel A. G. 59
  Jesse 63
Tucker, Carroll 62
  Dickson 54
  E. W. 74
  Elizabeth 67
  Elizabeth B. 74
  Enoch 61
  Jesse 39
  Martha 30, 33
  Nancy 22, 41
  Susan 25, 28, 51
  William 30
Tunnage, John 55
Turnborough, Nancy 37
Turnbow, James 47
  Thomas J. 67
Turner, Anne M. 6
  James A. 34
  Jane 62
  Lanetty 37
  Manerva J. 69
  Martha J. 46
  Matilda 42
  Nancy G. 62
  W. L. 27
  W. P. H. 70
Tutt, Hansford 16
  Richard B. 23
Tuttle, James 41
Tutts, Patience 23
Tyler, Sarah 54
  William 55
Underwood, George W. 58
  John B. 62, 63

Underwood (cont)
Mary 48
Uzzell, Martha A. 61
Sophia J. 62
Vails, Lucinda 72
Vandiver, Andrew C. 61
Ceneth 17
Cenith 31
Edward 33
Eliz L. 46
John H. 48
L. W. 64
Lucy Ann 60
P. B. 74
Sally 31
Sarah A. 56
Vatters, Alagany 26
Mirning 26
Vaughan, Balaam 61
William P. 44
Vaughn, Mary Ann 72
Mary E. 65
Vaughter, Alfy 38
Vawter, Nancy M. 46
Venable, Jane 20
Lucy 9
Vick, Alley T. 40
Benjamin J. 53
Elizabeth Ann 74
Vincent, Barbary 8
Sarah 29
Vinicent, Merriman 36
Voorhies, Angeline F. 32
Thomas 70
Vorhies, Angelina F. 36
Margaret M. 47
Martha E. 59
Rebecca Ann 41
Robert A. 58
Voss, Daniel 69
Eli 43
Elihu 41
Elizabeth Ann 71
Eveline 58
John 25, 41
Letty 23
Levi 48
Malinda 25
Martha E. 73
Mary 1
Mary Ann 74
Rebecca 73
Rebecca F. 30, 31
Sarah 64

Voss (cont)
Smith 38
Susan 55
Wiley 71
William 31
William H. 59
Votters, Cynthy 26
Waggoner, Thomas J. 25
Wagoner, Thomas 39
Waldrip, Joycey 19
Nancy 19
Prudy 19
Waldroup, Wm. 46
Walke, Letitia 24
Walker, Benjamin 45
Catharine 50
Eligah 13
Francis 24, 42
Lavina A. 60
Lucas 4
Martha Elizabeth 61
Mary 17
Permelia 45
Sally 19
Wm. R. 22, 24
William R. 42
Wall, Elizabeth M. 46
Jesse 70
John H. 66
Wallace, Bennett 1
Leticia 4
Malinda 18
Sarah Ann 62
Timothy 4
Wallis, Amy 5
Seneth 7
Wammack, Wiley 57
Ward, Sally 9
Warren, Angeline B. 8
Joel 29
John A. 61
Joseph L. 56
Lucy B. 23
Nancy 58
Robert N. 54
Warrick, C. K. 37
Warton, Mary Ann L. 46
Milly A. P. 55
Wasson, Caroline 38
Eli J. 36
Elizabeth C. 22
Elizabeth S. 9
Emeline A. 39
F. P. 41

Wasson (cont)
  J. F. 62
  James 14
  Lavina J. 22
  Margaret E. 72
  Martha A. 2
  Mary 70
  Mary J. 30
  Samuel M. 18, 32
  Sarah 40
  Susan M. 45
  W. N. 40
  William L. 32
Waters, Lisey 20
Watkins, Amelia A. 61
Watson, James W. 62
  Louisa 17
  Lucinda 61
  Martha J. 67
  Rebecca 49
  S. P. 69
  Suson 68
Weaver, America 71
  Christian 37
  Elizabeth 14, 63
  James 51
  James C. 60
  James R. 59
  Matthew 71
  Nancy 36
  Samuel 69
  Wilson 17
  Winney 59
Webb, A. J. E. 68
  Mary 71
  Ozias D. 74
  Susanna 16
Webster, James 11
  Nancy 11
Weeks, Prewet 35
Weir, Francis E. 7
Welch, Aseneth 7
  Elizabeth 29, 42
  James W. 55
  Jas. W. 70
  Jno. W. 35
  Levi 22
  Lucy 57
  Malinda 74
  Margaret 38
  Martha 54, 70
  Mary 53, 71
  Nicholas 42
  Sally 23

Welch (cont)
  Sarah 3
  Sarah M. 29
  William 5, 31
West, Martha C. 65
  Thomas 72
Wester, Elizabeth 42
  Fanny 23
  John 35
Wharton, Elizabeth 51
  Louise 51
  Nancy 10, 11
Wheeler, Mary Ann 56
  Thos. J. 43
White, Albert J. 58
  Albert J. M. 68
  Amanda E. 66
  Ann 45
  Daniel J. 65
  David H. 68
  Elender Jane 47
  Elisabeth 39
  Eliz M. 64
  Elizabeth 46
  Ephraim 40
  George 59
  Ira D. 71
  Isabela 71
  James J. 72
  James M. 70
  Jane 9, 11
  Johnathan 17
  Lucinda 38
  Lucy Jane 74
  Mahala 11
  Mahula 36
  Mahulda 63
  Malissa Ann 54
  Mary 54
  Nancy C. 56
  Raneney 43
  Sarah A. 56
  Sarah J. 74
  Wm. B. 67
Whitehead, Sarah 51
  Tobias A. 71
Whitley, A. N. 72
  Albert M. 66
  Alexander 52
Whittington, Malissa 55
Whitworth, Abraham 44, 49
  Jane 69
  Wm. 65
Wiggs, Amanda F. 49

Wiggs (cont)
Deely H. 5
Wilbourn, Adelia 52
Ananias 68
Wilburn, Sarah J. 71
Sarah Jane 71
Wilcockson, Eliz 63
Louisa J. 64
Wilcoxin, Sarah 46
Wiley, Alfred D. 50
Wilie, Isabella 15
Mary 20
Wilks, Lucey Ann 73
Willbourn, Jasper 50
Williams, Abner C. 39
Adaline 67
Alexander 69
Amanda 14
Bassil 58
Benjamin 28
Betsy 14
D. J. 70
David 45
Eleanor 41
Eliza 66
Elisabeth 43
Elizabeth 6
Fenner J. 40, 51
James 14, 54, 68
James C. R. 71
Jesse 31
Joel 66
John 52
John E. 66, 71
Lucinda E. 66
Mahulda 52
Manerva 41, 52
Martha 24, 59
Martha J. 75
Mary 28, 38, 65
Mary Ann 62
Mary J. 72
Melvina 39
Nancy 53
Nancy A. 58
Nancy N. 46
Preston 65
Rebecca R. 50
Robert B. 58
Robt. 42
Saphronia 69
Sarah 47
Sarah M. 44
Susannah C. 55

Williams (cont)
Thomas N. 40
W. A. 26
Wm. B. 74
William H. 54
Williamson, Sophia 5
Willis, Alphonso 54
Caroline M. 6
James V. 67
Malachi 42
Moses H. 50
Willoughby, Sally 34
Wilsford, Alitka 37
Amanda 41
Angeline 61
George W. 62
Granville T. 50
Thomas 48
Wilson, Dice 67
E. B. 70
Henry S. 32
John 63
Wimpy, Matilda R. M. 26
R. M. 26
Winn, Wm. 18
Winters, Edward 74
Moses 9
Rebecca 9
Wisdom, A. B. 60
Elizabeth 17, 18
Francis M. 64
Harriet 25
Lenora P. 55
Margaret 39
Nancy 18, 31
Sally 16
Sarah 7
Susan M. 66
Thomas 16
William N. 42
Wm. W. 9
Wise, Mary Ann 38
Wolf, Charles H. 49
Womack, Newton C. 18
Wood, Benjamin 47
Hannah 52
John 45
L. L. 38
Margaret R. 73
Margret K. 41
Reuben 62
Solomon 43, 64
Solomon L. 9
Stephen L. 63

Woodard, Matilda 12
  Moses 18
Woods, Easter 13
  Lucy 42
  Perny 8
Wooten, Mary E. 53
Workman, R. C. 38
Wortham, Alex S. 38
  Cornelia J. 45
  Julia A. 34
Wright, Martha 70
  Moses 69
  P. M. 73
  Period 7
  Perrin 71
Wynick, Anna 35
Wyrick, Anna 4
  George W. 13
Yancey, Thomas 34
Yancy, John 67
  Malissa Jane 41
Yarbough, Narcissa 70
  Polly 11
Yates, Tyre R. 59
  Tyree 11
Yearwood, William 36
Yeomans, Mahaly 17
Yomans, Eady 17
York, Elisabeth 39
  James 51
  Sarah 53
  Susannah 7
Young, G. D. 12
  Lucy A. 52
Younger, Rebecca 69

www.ingramcontent.com/pod-product-compliance
Lightning Source LLC
Chambersburg PA
CBHW072205270326
41930CB00011B/2538